# VERY WEDNESDAY

*The Extraordinary and Unprecedented 2019/20 Season*

Louis Paul Shackshaft

# DISCLAIMER

This book is unofficial and is not in any way affiliated or associated with Sheffield Wednesday Football Club or its employees. The information in this book is based on the author's knowledge, experience and opinion; it is not in any way meant to purge, humiliate or defame anyone. The publisher and author assume no responsibility for errors, inaccuracies, omissions or any other inconsistencies herein. The use of this book therefore implies your acceptance of this disclaimer.

*This book is dedicated to the memory of my close friend and life-long Sheffield Wednesday fan Ash Prendergast. The fantastic memories of us both supporting the Owls together will stay with me forever. He was loved by all and will never be forgotten.*

*(Ashley Jon Edward Prendergast 4th February 1984 - 3rd April 2020)*

# CONTENTS

# INTRODUCTION

Sheffield Wednesday have a proud history having won four First Division Championships, three FA Cups, one League Cup and one Community Shield, amongst other accolades. Formed in 1867 and as one of the oldest football clubs in the world, Wednesday entered a new decade within the 2019/20 campaign.

In modern times the Owls have had many ups and more downs since their relegation from the Premier League at the end of the 1999/2000 season. Even though this millennium hasn't been too kind to Wednesday, every new season brings renewed hope and opportunity. The Owls now find themselves as a reputable Championship side having spent eight-years in this division since their promotion from League One in 2012.

Former Chairman Milan Mandaric and current Chairman Dejphon Chansiri have both been responsible for playing integral parts in the club's sustainability, infrastructure and development since 2010.

At the start of the 2019/20 season, the difficult fight back towards the promised land continued as Sheffield Wednesday aimed for a top-half finish. Remember, at the turn of each new decade for the past forty-nine-years the Owls have suffered four relegations (1969/70, 1989/90, 1999/00, 2009/10) and gained one promotion (1979/80). The big question was whether or not this trend would be sustained?

In a division as competitive and unforgiving as the Championship, would the forthcoming campaign turn out to be a success or one that was riddled with adversity and misfortune? Like the flip of a coin the Owls could easily ascend to the right or descend to the wrong end of the league table.

Meanwhile, Wednesdayites could only watch and wait whilst fine margins played a pivotal role in the outcome of the Owls' future.

Step into the world of a Sheffield Wednesday fan and relive the emotional highs and lows of the Owls' pre-season, managerial departures, appointments, transfer windows, suspensions, looming misconduct charges, the coronavirus pandemic, player contributions, statistics and much more.

This is the extraordinary and unprecedented 2019/20 season...

# PRE-SEASON

*Expect The Unexpected*

Following the end of the 2018/19 season, Steve Bruce was tasked with releasing players who he felt were surplus to requirements and alternatively offer new deals to those he felt justified an extended stay.

Amongst an endless list of senior pros that were released during the summer, Gary Hooper was the most notable. The Sheffield Wednesday number fourteen had spent the majority of the season side-lined through injury and was consequently shown the exit door.

As ever during the excitement of a summer transfer window, questions remained over the extent in which the Owls would explore the market for recruitment purposes. For the first time in a few years Sheffield Wednesday had to be shrewd whilst conducting their transfer business due to a soft but on-going transfer embargo. Players from the free and loan markets looked the more likely targets. In the meantime, it was believed that Bruce was also looking to offload a couple of players from the current squad for costly fees if possible.

The first confirmed deal of the summer was on the 9th July when Keiren Westwood penned a two-year stay. This news was met with both joy and relief after the Wednesday shot-stopper had supposedly been linked with a move away from the club, this was because of his demotion earlier in the season under Jos Luhukay.

Sheffield Wednesday's longest servant Liam Palmer also secured a contract extension on the 12th July after signing a three-year deal until 2022. Palmer had recently made his international debut for Scotland and was a stand-out performer for the Owls towards the back end of the 2018/19 term.

Kieran Lee was the final prominent player to sign on the dotted line on the 26th July, he'd lengthened his stay for another twelve-months. Regardless of the thirty-one-year-old only playing seventy-minutes of first team football during the 2018/19 campaign through injury, Lee was still a very able midfielder and was judged as a risk worth taking.

In terms of incomings, Steve Bruce remained focused on strengthening the positions that now lacked in numbers and had therefore weakened; attention was primarily set on the defence and the wider areas of midfield.

Upon hearing the pleasant news that the current transfer embargo was to be lifted in due course, Owls fans remained poised as three rumoured transfer targets looked set to arrive. Sheffield Wednesday then signed all three of these players in as many days.

Julian Börner was the first onset on the 10$^{th}$ July. The twenty-eight-year-old former German youth international was a centre-back and arrived on a free from Arminia Bielefeld where he had been club captain.

Just twenty-four-hours later, Börner was followed through the door by Brentford's Moses Odubajo, he too was a free transfer. The twenty-five-year-old had bags of English football league experience at right-back and this was a position in which the Wednesday squad was yearning for.

The third and final signing prior to the season commencing was Kadeem Harris on the 13$^{th}$ July; the pacey winger had arrived at Hillsborough from Cardiff City, also on a free. The twenty-six-year-old former Bluebird would now act as healthy competition in wide areas for the likes of Adam Reach and Fernando Forestieri, to name a few.

On the field, Sheffield Wednesday remained in good spirit having won three consecutive pre-season friendlies in a row. The first practice match took place at the Estadio da Nora in Portugal on the 9$^{th}$ July, the Owls beat Shrewsbury Town two-nil thanks to goals from Lucas Joao and Sam Winnall.

Just days later on the 13$^{th}$ July, Wednesday were victorious against both Lincoln City and Stocksbridge Park Steels, winning three-one and five-nil respectively. Jordan Rhodes, Adam Reach and a Neal Eardley own goal sealed the win for Wednesday in the earlier kick-off at Sincil Bank. The following Owls, Sam Winnall, Kadeem Harris, Atdhe Nuhiu, Fernando Forestieri and Joost van Aken all netted in the later kick-off at Bracken Moor.

Despite the fact that pre-season remained buoyant so far in terms of results on and off the pitch, lifelong Wednesday enthusiasts have learnt over time to take the rough with the smooth and to expect the unexpected in equal measures. With that in mind, developing theories suggested that Newcastle United Chairman Mike Ashley favoured Steve Bruce for his unoccupied managerial role at Newcastle United.

As the gossip and speculation began to grow, everyone was under the impression that Bruce's short reign at Sheffield Wednesday may be over.

Then it was confirmed...

## Steve Bruce Departure

You cannot mention Sheffield Wednesday's 2019/20 campaign without referring to the managerial disarray that left the club in limbo.

Pre-season was hugely disrupted on the 15$^{th}$ July when

Steve Bruce resigned from his managerial post amid reports suggesting he was to step into the vacant role at Newcastle United, succeeding Rafael Benitez. Stepping down with Bruce were his assistants Steve Agnew and Stephen Clemence who would both make the journey to the north-east also.

Fifty-eight-year-old Bruce had only been in charge of the Owls since January and guided Wednesday to a twelfth place finish in the Championship that season. He was victorious in seven of his eighteen fixtures, losing on three occasions.

Bruce's vast experience at this level and his connections within the footballing network displayed signs of stability and promise for the 2019/20 term; nevertheless, his departure put a serious dent in preparations ahead of the new campaign.

Due to private circumstances and after a four-week delay, Steve Bruce had only been officially appointed as the Sheffield Wednesday boss on the 1st February 2019. Bruce was granted his wish by the Owls Chairman to postpone his start date so he could attend to matters of a personal nature. It was reasons such as this as to why many of the Wednesday faithful were left outraged at the manner in which Bruce appeared to arrange his departure from Hillsborough just five-months later.

Nobody could deny Bruce of this opportunity or argue with the fact that it was his dream was to manage his boyhood club. Yet given the fact that Sheffield Wednesday Chairman showed nothing but compassion and thoughtfulness ahead of Bruce's appointment with the Owls, this was an irritating state of affairs for everyone associated with the club.

The situation soon went from bad to worse as it became apparent that legal issues were still unresolved between the two sides in question. A dispute was now on-going over the former Owls boss.

With only nineteen-days before Wednesday's first competitive clash against Reading, Dejphon Chansiri was left with a huge predicament. Should he appoint a permanent manager within a handful of days, or wait and leave the trustworthy Lee Bullen in the caretaker role?

## Lee 'Dependable' Bullen

With little time to gather his thoughts surrounding the Steve Bruce palaver, Lee Bullen found himself as the Sheffield Wednesday caretaker for the third time in his coaching career.

The Scottish cult hero previously made one-hundred and forty-eight competitive appearances for Sheffield Wednesday between 2004 and 2008 and was part of the Owls 2004/05 League One promotion winning side via the play-offs. In later life, Bullen had been with the Wednesday management staff since 2011 in youth coach, development head coach and assistant manager roles, aiding Stuart Gray, Carlos Carvalhal, Jos Luhukay and Steve Bruce during their endeavours.

With an indispensable amount of experience at the club and having spent thirteen-years at Hillsborough in total so far, Lee also possesses the priceless trait of wearing his heart on his sleeve. Still, it was time to act fast. Bullen only had a couple of weeks to formulate a strategy and ensure his players remained focussed ahead of the opening day fixture at Reading. Even so, this was going to be a tough ask with all of the on-going disruption off of the field.

Forty-eight-year-old Bullen had a win record of thirty-seven-percent from his previous eight games in temporary charge of the Owls, winning three, drawing three and losing on two occasions. His last and most notable victory was Wednesday's one-nil victory at Middlesbrough on Boxing Day 2018.

Due to the nature of Steve Bruce's sudden departure, speculation suggested that Bullen, who had been very dependable when called upon, may be appointed the manager of Sheffield Wednesday on a full time basis, particularly if he was successful in his on-going custodian role.

While many names were thrown around for the current vacant management position, there were no front runners once Chris Hughton was rumoured to have ruled himself out of the job. The key question remained, was Bullen the right man for the job and would he be given a fair crack at the whip? The Wednesday Chairman had a lot to contemplate before making his final decision.

As the launch of the new season was drawing even closer and without any confirmed appointment, it appeared that Lee was going to be given the opportunity he had been craving for.

Ahead of the opening trip to Reading, Sheffield Wednesday still had four pre-season friendlies to endure in Bullen's safekeeping. First of all, the Owls managed to surpass Northampton Town in a four-nil win on the 16th July. Adam Reach, Steven Fletcher, Atdhe Nuhiu and Jordan Rhodes were all on the score-sheet that day.

Days later on a quick pre-season tour of Germany, Wednesday were defeated one-nil by VfB Lubeck on the 19th July. They then turned around a two-nil deficit to win three-two against Holstein Kiel on the 21st July. Jordan Rhodes scored to spark the Owls comeback before Steven Fletcher notched twice in the second-half.

In the final pre-season friendly before the regular campaign, Sheffield Wednesday drew two-a-piece with Spanish outfit Espanyol on the 28th July at Hillsborough. Steven Fletcher and Fernando Forestieri got the goals.

At that point and with another British summer almost over, the pre-season pandemonium had quickly come to a close.

# VERY WEDNESDAY

*The 2019/20 Campaign*

As Lee Bullen continued with full responsibility of the first-team, the competitive nature of the Championship was now in sight. Sheffield Wednesday fans braced themselves ahead of the new season...

**3pm Saturday 3rd August, The Madejski Stadium (Attendance: 16,319)**

**Reading 1-3 Sheffield Wednesday** (Harris 30', Meite 54', Hutchinson 56', Westwood Sent Off 80', Joao 90+7')

The 2019/20 season couldn't have started any better for Lee Bullen and his Owls as they took all three points on the opening day.

Kadeem Harris stole the show with a glittering performance out wide, his pace and ability to beat a man was everything the fans had been hoping for.

On the half-hour mark, he glided past one defender before slipping the ball beyond Neves Virginia to give Wednesday the lead. It was a fantastic solo effort.

Reading found an equaliser not long into the second-half when Yakou Meite delicately looped his header over Keiren Westwood.

Just two-minutes later and with the tie locked at one-all, Sam Hutchinson stepped up to power a header home from a Barry Bannan corner. The holding-mid-fielder's celebration didn't disappoint either as he ran towards the away stand like a man possessed.

Keiren Westwood was sent off when he rushed out to clear the ball with ten-minutes remaining. He had up-ended Mo Barrow who would've been clear through on goal. Despite having the extra man, the home side continued to press but to no avail.

With only seconds remaining in added-time, Lucas Joao sealed the win with an outstanding swivelling effort from twenty-yards. That was three points in the bag.

The Owls had now won back-to-back away league outings versus Reading for the first time in forty-years. What a start to the season that was. At 5pm, Sheffield Wednesday were sat at the top of the table, temporarily.

**League position:** 2nd

**Reading starting eleven:** Virgínia, Yiadom, Moore, Miazga, Richards, Loader (Adam 65'), Rinomhota, Swift (Novakovich 85'), Barrett (Olise 65'), Barrow, Meite.

**Sheffield Wednesday starting eleven:** Westwood, Odubajo, Lees, Börner, Palmer, Lee (Joao 78'), Hutchinson, Bannan, Reach, Fletcher (Dawson 82'), Harris (Forestieri 78').

## The Countdown To Deadline Day

A few days prior to the deadline on the 6th August, Lucas Joao secured a permanent transfer to Reading for an undisclosed fee that was believed to be in the region of £5 million. Ironically, Joao's goal against the Royals just three-days earlier was his final contribution for Sheffield Wednesday.

Also on the same day and as business began to heat up across the nation, the Owls captured the signing of experienced goalkeeper Paul Jones on a free transfer from Fleetwood Town. Jones arrived as backup cover for Westwood and Dawson because Joe Wildsmith faced a lengthy period on the side-lines due to a knee injury.

When deadline day arrived on the 8th August 2019, Massimo Luongo became Sheffield Wednesday's next and fifth acquisition of the window. The Australian born box-to-box midfielder arrived at Hillsborough from Championship challengers Queens Park Rangers for an undisclosed fee.

Later that day, two additional players were welcomed on season-long-loans. The Owls acquired winger Jacob Murphy from Newcastle United to enhance competition for places out wide. The final signing of the window was centre-back David Bates; the twenty-two-year-old Scottish defender had been attained from German outfit Hamburger SV.

As the permanent transfer window slammed shut, the Owls had conducted intelligent business trades; capturing seven first-team signatures in total. Wednesday now had strength and depth in most positions throughout the squad.

Thanks to the sale of Lucas Joao for a pricey sum, expenditure was low during the transfer frame which was crucial from a commercial perspective and its current profit and sustainability rules.

Overall it rang true that this had been a very fruitful window. However, it wasn't quite over just yet. Once deadline day had past, four players temporarily departed the club on loan deals.

Midfielder Connor Kirby made the geographically short trip to Macclesfield Town when he secured his move on the 9th August. Then, Joost van Aken joined VFL Osnabruck just five-days later and it wasn't until later in the month when winger Jack Stobbs joined Scottish side Livingston on the 20th August.

The final and most eye-catching loan deal of them all

was Matt Penney's. The twenty-one-year-old teamed up with the former Owls boss Jos Luhukay at German club FC St. Pauli on the 22$^{nd}$ August. Luhukay had handed Penney his Sheffield Wednesday debut in a League Cup tie against Sunderland in the 2018/19 season. Many Wednesdayites were now keen to see how this arrangement transformed for the full-back.

## The 2019/20 Campaign Continued…

### 3pm Saturday 10$^{th}$ August, Hillsborough (Attendance: 28,028)

### Sheffield Wednesday 2-0 Barnsley (Murphy 2', Fletcher 60')

The Owls continued their unbeaten start to the season with victory in the South Yorkshire derby at Hillsborough.

Once again it was another debutant who stole the headlines; Jacob Murphy gave Wednesday an early lead with his first touch of the ball when he slotted home with an instep finish.

Barnsley were up for the fight and should've been level when Cauley Woodrow fired towards goal from close range, only for Cameron Dawson to pull off a stunning reflex save.

It was in the second-half when Steven Fletcher guaranteed Wednesday maximum points. On the hour, the Scottish front-man created space for a shot and drilled the ball directly into the right-sided corner of the goal. That was the killer blow for the visitors.

Not long after, Julian Börner captured the hearts of many Owls fans when he instinctively celebrated a goal-line clearance.

At the final whistle, Sheffield Wednesday had won their first opening two fixtures for the first time since the 1996/97 campaign and remained unbeaten versus Barnsley in eleven league matches. The Owls jumped to summit of the table, albeit on goal difference.

**League position:** 1st

**Sheffield Wednesday starting eleven:** Dawson, Odubajo, Lees, Börner, Palmer, Lee (Luongo 80'), Hutchinson, Reach, Murphy (Pelupessy 74'), Fletcher (Rhodes 77'), Harris.

**Barnsley starting eleven:** Radlinger, Sibbick, Diaby, Andersen, Cavaré, McGeehan, Mowatt (Styles 77'), Thomas, Bähre (Chaplin 61'), Wilks (Thiam 62'), Woodrow.

**3pm Saturday 17$^{th}$ August, The Den (Attendance: 15,017)**

**Millwall 1-0 Sheffield Wednesday** (Smith 37', Wallace Sent Off 43')

It was Millwall who maintained their unbeaten run in the Championship after grinding out a win against Sheffield Wednesday with only ten men.

Adam Reach tried his luck with a spectacular effort from thirty-yards on the right, it would've been an outrageous goal but his shot was just an inch or so too high and it grazed the top of the crossbar.

As the Lions pressed, Matt Smith scored the only goal of the game from a corner. After a sloppy defensive mix-up, Keiren Westwood failed to claim the ball before the target-man nodded home.

Jed Wallace was sent-off just before half-time for a mistimed tackle on Kieran Lee. This gave Wednesday a glimmer of hope as the sides returned for the remaining forty-five-minutes but the visitors failed to capitalise with the extra man.

Regardless of having twenty-one shots at goal in total, the Owls fell short in this contest and suffered their first defeat of the season.

**League position:** 6th

**Millwall starting eleven:** Bialkowski, Romeo, Pearce, Cooper, Wallace, Mahoney (Leonard 74'), Thompson,

Williams, Wallace, O'Brien (Ferguson 83'), Smith (Bradshaw 52').

**Sheffield Wednesday starting eleven:** Westwood, Iorfa (Bannan 45'), Lees, Börner, Palmer (Luongo 59'), Reach, Hutchinson, Lee (Rhodes 65'), Murphy, Fletcher, Harris.


**7.45pm Tuesday 20<sup>th</sup> August, Hillsborough (Attendance: 23,353)**

**Sheffield Wednesday 1-0 Luton Town** (Harris 54')

Sheffield Wednesday were back to winning ways in what was their first mid-week tie of the season.

Whilst the first-half performance was nothing to shout about, it was Kadeem Harris who made the breakthrough in the second-half. Steven Fletcher nodded the ball towards the back post and Harris made no mistake on the goal-line.

Summer recruit Julian Börner thought he'd helped double the Owls advantage when his cushioned header was finished off by Fletcher; though the marksman was judged to be offside.

Westwood was a spectator for most of the match as Luton offered very little up top. The one goal was enough thanks to a dogged second-half display.

This victory ensured the Owls had maintained their one-hundred-percent home win record this term and they had still only lost two of their last twenty-two fixtures on a Tuesday night at Hillsborough.

**League position:** 4th

**Sheffield Wednesday starting eleven:** Westwood, Odubajo, Lees, Börner, Fox, Hutchinson, Bannan, Murphy, Reach (Winnall 78'), Harris (Lee 88'), Fletcher (Luongo 85').

**Luton Town starting eleven:** Sluga, Cranie (Bolton 59'), Pearson, Bradley, Bree, Butterfield (Mpanzu 74'), Shinnie, Tunnicliffe, Collins, LuaLua (Brown 69'), Cornick.

**3pm Saturday 24th August, Deepdale (Attendance: 15,715)**

**Preston North-End 2-1 Sheffield Wednesday** (Johnson Penalty 32', Johnson Penalty 65', Fletcher 78')

Preston North-End converted penalty kicks in either half of the tie to defeat the Owls.

Moses Odubajo had a game to forget as he brought down Sean Maguire inside the area on two separate occasions. Daniel Johnson converted the first even though Westwood did get a hand to it, the ball had crept into the bottom corner and he was unlucky not to make the save.

Johnson notched his second midway through the second-half when he replicated his initial spot-kick by shooting right. Westwood had dived the wrong way this time so that was two-nil to the hosts. Wednesday now had a mountain to climb.

The Owls did manage to pull a goal back as the contest edged closer to full-time when Adam Reach drifted a cross into the path of Fletcher, running onto the ball the marksman then headed past the stranded Declan Rudd.

Wednesday pushed for the equaliser but Preston managed to hold on for the win, both sides were level on nine points at full-time.

**League position:** 9th

**Preston North-End starting eleven:** Rudd, Fisher, Bauer (Storey 62'), Davies, Rafferty, Pearson, Browne, Bodin (Barkhuizen 58'), Johnson (Gallagher 85'), Maguire, Stockley.

**Sheffield Wednesday starting eleven:** Westwood, Odubajo (Reach 66'), Lees, Börner, Fox, Lee (Nuhiu 72'), Hutchinson, Bannan, Murphy (Forestieri 45'), Fletcher, Harris.

**Carabao Cup Round Two - 7.45pm Wednesday 28<sup>th</sup> August, New York Stadium (Attendance: 8,679)**

**Rotherham United 0-1 Sheffield Wednesday** (Nuhiu 90+6')

A last-gasp winning effort by Atdhe Nuhiu saw Wednesday reach the third round of the Carabao Cup.

Having received a bye in the first round due to Bury's potential dismissal from the English Football League, the Owls made the short South Yorkshire trip.

Lee Bullen made numerous changes ahead of this fixture, most notably with loanee David Bates and newcomer Massimo Luongo making the starting eleven.

With no goals and very little between the sides during the ninety, a penalty shoot-out was looking increasingly likely. However, Wednesday continued to press and had to wait until the final moments before securing progression into the next round.

After scrapping to get to the ball, it was the 'giant' Kosovan who prodded home from a Kadeem Harris cross.

Confirming victory in the final seconds had become a common theme for the Owls recently against their South Yorkshire challengers.

Wednesday would now face Everton at Hillsborough in the third round.

**Rotherham United starting eleven:** Iversen, Olosunde, Ihiekwe, Wood, Robertson, Wiles, Barlaser (MacDonald 67'), Crooks (Lindsay 61'), Ladapo, Smith (Proctor 74'), Vassell.

**Sheffield Wednesday starting eleven:** Dawson, Iorfa, Bates, Thorniley, Fox, Murphy (Bannan 65'), Pelupessy (Forestieri 76'), Luongo, Winnall (Harris 45'), Rhodes, Nuhiu.

**3pm Saturday 31st August, Hillsborough (Attendance: 23,446)**

**Sheffield Wednesday 1-2 Queens Park Rangers** (Fletcher 23', Hugill 60', Hugill 64')

A second-half Jordan Hugill brace wrapped up all the points for QPR as they came from behind to clinch the win.

In this final fixture before the international break, it was the home side that managed to get their noses in front thanks to a dubious decision that saw Forestieri tussled to the ground. There was no hesitation from the referee who quickly pointed to the spot. Steven Fletcher took aim and coolly converted from twelve-yards.

It was then on the hour when Hugill grabbed his first goal of the game, after beating the offside trap he rounded Westwood and finished with ease. Only four-minutes later he poked home again to turn the tie in favour of the visitors.

Wednesday gave it a good go in segments but were unable to find a leveller. Atdhe Nuhiu did manage to get on the end of a Barry Bannan delivery but his unorthodox effort hit the side netting.

At full-time the Owls had suffered their first two successive league defeats of the season. Regrettably for Lee Bullen also, this contest turned out to be his final game in charge as caretaker boss.

**League position:** 11th

**Sheffield Wednesday starting eleven:** Westwood, Palmer (Murphy 75'), Iorfa, Börner, Fox (Luongo 67'), Reach (Nuhiu 76'), Hutchinson, Bannan, Harris, Forestieri, Fletcher.

**Queens Park Rangers starting eleven:** Lumley, Rangel (Kane 88'), Hall, Leistner, Barbet, Manning, Eze (Scowen 83'), Ball, Chair, Hugill, Wells (Mlakar 67').

# Fernando Forestieri Banned

Fans favourite Fernando Forestieri was officially banned for six matches on the 5th September 2019 by the Football Association's independent regulatory commission after his appeal was dismissed.

This saga had been an on-going affair since July 2018 when Sheffield Wednesday had travelled to Mansfield

Town in a pre-season friendly. The five-foot-eight-inch forward was accused of using racist language towards Stags defender Krystian Pearce in an incident that ended in a scuffle involving players and staff from both sides.

To add salt to the wounds, the Owls number forty-five was previously acquitted in March 2019 at the Mansfield Magistrates Court but still received a £25,000 fine in addition to his lengthy ban by the FA.

Consequently, Forestieri would be unavailable for the upcoming six competitive fixtures. These included Huddersfield Town, Fulham, Everton, Middlesbrough, Hull City and Wigan Athletic. His next availability for selection would be on Friday the 18th October when Sheffield Wednesday travel to Cardiff City.

Whilst the Wednesday faithful may have felt Forestieri's further punishment was unjust, his presence in the match-day squad had become very irregular. He had struggled to hold down a regular spot in the Owls' first-team because of minor injuries and heavy competition for places in the forward line. The tricky play-maker had only made it to the starting eleven once so far this term in addition to a couple of appearances from the bench.

Since his arrival from Watford in the summer of 2015, Fernando had been a servant at the club for over four-years. All the same, his contract was due to expire at the end of the campaign. Game time was crucial for Forestieri if he was to remain on the Owls' books beyond the current 2019/20 season.

With that in mind, as Dejphon Chansiri continued to search for a new gaffer to succeed Steve Bruce, within twenty-four-hours it was confirmed that Garry Monk was the man that the little Argentinian must excite in the next eight-months, if he was to remain a Wednesday player.

# GARRY MONK APPOINTMENT

*The Transition*

On Friday 6th September, Garry Monk was appointed the new Sheffield Wednesday boss; ending speculation that Lee Bullen may have taken charge of the Owls on a permanent basis.

Dejphon Chansiri's decision to recruit during the international break was probably a wise move even though this arrangement came somewhat out of the blue.

Only a few days prior to Monk's arrival it was believed that Danny Cowley was the man who looked set to fill the vacant role. Most Wednesday fans were beginning to come to terms with this speculation due to his successful back-to-back promotions with Lincoln City in the lower leagues.

Nevertheless, despite Cowley and Monk both being

British, forty-years of age and with bags of potential, questions were raised over the Imps' boss due to his lack of experience in the top-tiers of English football. Monk had also previously worked under and had a understanding of financial fair play implications, this was a common topic at S6 in recent years due to a couple of soft transfer embargoes. As a result, Dejphon Chansiri opted for the ex-Birmingham City chief.

As well as Cowley, there were other managers that looked likely to be in the hot-seat before Monk's position was confirmed. Lee Bullen, Tony Pulis and Gary Rowett were all rumoured to be in with a shout, but in the end this was all proven to be just hearsay.

Monk arrived at Hillsborough with a handful of fully-fledged Championship years under his belt and boosted a win record of thirty-nine-percent during his reign at four former clubs. He had previously managed Birmingham City, Middlesbrough and Leeds United; he was also the boss of Swansea City in the Premier League. Additionally, Monk was a centre-back in his playing days and made fifteen appearances for the Owls between 2002 and 2003 on loan from Southampton.

The news of Garry Monk's onset confirmed that Lee Bullen's hope of the permanent appointment had vanished. Still, his long-established career as part of the managerial staff would continue in the fundamental assistant manager role to his new superior. Nonetheless, Bullen's overseer position certainly didn't go unnoticed as he played an integral part to Sheffield Wednesday's decent start to the season. He was victorious in four of his seven ties at the helm.

Coincidently, with only nine-days remaining before the Owls' trip to Huddersfield Town, Danny Cowley was appointed the new Terriers boss. Both recently hired foremen would now be sat in either dug-out on Sunday.

In many ways, as Sheffield Wednesday entered a new chapter under Garry Monk, the season would start now for the Owls as the transition began to unfold.

## The 2019/20 Campaign Continued…

**12pm Sunday 15th September, The John Smith's Stadium (Attendance: 22,754)**

**Huddersfield Town 0-2 Sheffield Wednesday** (Fletcher 10', Winnall 72')

Garry Monk made a winning start as he came head-to-head with Danny Cowley in the clash between the newly appointed managers.

With ten-minutes gone, Kadeem Harris showed some neat footwork on the left and his subsequent cross was finished off by Steven Fletcher with his head. That was his third goal in three successive fixtures, a feat he hadn't previously managed to achieve in seven-years.

In the second-half and thanks to a shrewd substitution by Monk, it was Sam Winnall who guaranteed Wednesday the victory. His glancing header went in off the post from a perfect Barry Bannan delivery. That was his first goal for the Owls since December 2017; Winnall had finally managed to take advantage of the opportunity he had been longing for.

The recent history books also suggested that the hosts would find it difficult to score. Town came at the Owls but they were restricted to only a couple of hopeful efforts. Soon after, the referee called for full-time.

This result confirmed an unbeaten record versus Huddersfield Town in ten successive fixtures. In addition, the Owls had not conceded a single goal in eight contests at the John Smith's stadium. That's thirteen-hours and three-minutes to be exact. Unbelievable!

**League position:** 9th

**Huddersfield Town starting eleven:** Grabara, Hadergjonaj, Elphick, Schindler, Kongolo, Chalobah, Hogg, O'Brien (Bacuna 66'), Diakhaly (Mbenza 56'), Campbell (Mounie 77'), Grant.

**Sheffield Wednesday starting eleven:** Westwood, Odubajo, Iorfa, Börner, Palmer, Hutchinson, Bannan, Murphy (Winnall 60'), Reach, Harris (Lee 86'), Fletcher (Nuhiu 83').

**3pm Saturday 21st September, Hillsborough (Attendance: 23,342)**

**Sheffield Wednesday 1-1 Fulham** (Cairney 42', Nuhiu 90+3')

A stoppage-time header from Atdhe Nuhiu salvaged a point for the Owls in what was Garry Monk's first game in charge at Hillsborough.

Fulham took the lead just before half-time when Keiren Westwood parried a cross into the path of Tom Cairney, who then slotted home from eight-yards.

Although it was the visitors who had the majority of the possession, Wednesday were creating the better openings in front of goal.

The equaliser came courtesy of a deflected Kadeem Harris cross which fell into the path of Nuhiu, the colossal front-man threw himself forward and headed the ball into the bottom right corner of the goal. One-all!

The goal sparked huge celebrations, more so at the relief of a draw when only moments earlier a home defeat looked inevitable. Both of Atdhe Nuhiu's goals this term had now come in added-time.

This was Sheffield Wednesday's first draw of the campaign and Garry Monk had also maintained his unbeaten record in five head-to-heads versus Fulham as a manager, winning once and drawing four times.

The Owls now found themselves two points off the

play-offs and only four points behind Leeds United, who were sat at the top of the table.

**League position:** 8th

**Sheffield Wednesday starting eleven:** Westwood, Odubajo, Iorfa, Börner, Palmer, Hutchinson, Reach (Murphy 59'), Lee (Winnall 70'), Bannan, Harris, Fletcher (Nuhiu 77').

**Fulham starting eleven:** Bettinelli, Sessegnon (Odoi 67'), Mawson, Ream, Bryan, De-Cordova Reid, Reed, Cairney, Knockaert (Kamara 83'), Mitrovic, Cavaliero (Arter 66').

**Carabao Cup Round Three - 7.45pm Tuesday 24th September, Hillsborough (Attendance: 21,485)**

**Sheffield Wednesday 0-2 Everton** (Calvert-Lewin 6', Calvert-Lewin 10')

It was Everton who progressed to the League Cup fourth round thanks to a Dominic Calvert-Lewin brace inside the opening ten-minutes.

Only Moses Odubajo, Dominic Iorfa and Adam Reach retained their place in the starting eleven after Wednesday's recent score draw with Fulham.

These eight changes all but confirmed Monk's priority was in the league this season, yet it was the home side that should've probably found themselves one-nil up inside the first two-minutes. Sam Winnall pounced on a poor back pass by Tom Davies but his effort was wonderfully saved by Jordan Pickford.

Moments later, the Owls were made to pay for their earlier miss when Calvert-Lewis slammed home a volley past Cameron Dawson. The Sheffield born forward then grabbed his second goal with a simple tap-in from an Alex Iwobi cut-back.

As Wednesday continued to press for a goal, Dominic Iorfa came closest when he headed wide at the back post when it probably seemed easier to score.

At full-time, this was Garry Monk's first competitive defeat since taking charge of the Owls. However, despite the disappointment of a cup exit, this result may have come as a blessing in disguise...

**Sheffield Wednesday starting eleven:** Dawson, Odubajo, Iorfa, Thorniley, Fox, Reach, Pelupessy, Luongo, Murphy (Harris 59'), Winnall (Rhodes 65'), Nuhiu (Fletcher 70').

**Everton starting eleven:** Pickford, Sidibe, Mina, Holgate, Digne, Davies, Delph (Schneiderlin 90+1'), Richarlison (Walcott 67'), Iwobi, Bernard (Sigurdsson 76'), Calvert-Lewin.

**3pm Saturday 28th September, Riverside Stadium (Attendance: 22,075)**

**Middlesbrough 1-4 Sheffield Wednesday** (Clayton Own Goal 5', Iorfa 6', McNair 19', Reach 23', Fletcher 34')

Sheffield Wednesday secured their biggest victory of the campaign so far as Garry Monk made a return to one of his former clubs.

The Owls ran riot in the first-half when all of their goals came in the opening thirty-four-minutes. An Adam Clayton own-goal set Wednesday on their way, then seconds later Dominic Iorfa scored with a header from a Barry Bannan set-piece.

Paddy McNair buried a shot for the hosts just before the travelling side grabbed a third. Adam Reach found the corner of Darren Randolph's goal from eighteen-yards after a neat pass from Atdhe Nuhiu. Wednesday were three-one up with over sixty-five-minutes of the tie left to play.

The Owls then put the contest beyond Boro and it was Adam Reach who played a significant part once again; he drifted a cross into the path of Steven Fletcher who headed down and into the goal. That was Wednesday's eighth headed goal of the season which was more than any other Championship side at the time.

The Owls managed to see out the second-half without concern and when the full-time whistle blew, Wednesday had closed in on the final play-off spot. This was one hell of an away day for those who had made the journey to the Riverside Stadium.

This result confirmed the Owls first back-to-back league win versus Middlesbrough since 1991. Furthermore, this victory was also Garry Monk's first win versus Middlesbrough since his departure from the club in 2017.

**League position:** 7th

**Middlesbrough starting eleven:** Randolph, Dijksteel, Shotton, Fry, Bola (Ayala 45'), McNair, Wing, Clayton (Browne 45'), Johnson (Walker 74'), Fletcher, Assombalonga.

**Sheffield Wednesday starting eleven:** Westwood, Odubajo, Iorfa, Börner, Palmer, Hutchinson (Luongo 41'), Bannan, Reach, Harris (Fox 89'), Nuhiu (Winnall 80'), Fletcher.

**7.45pm Tuesday 1st October, KCOM Stadium (Attendance: 11,590)**

**Hull City 1-0 Sheffield Wednesday** (Eaves 72')

Garry Monk suffered his first league defeat of the season at the KCOM Stadium.

The best opening of the forty-five fell to Atdhe Nuhiu from a Barry Bannan cross, even though he had more time than he realised his effort drifted wide of the post.

Substitute Tom Eaves secured the points for the hosts in the second period when he neatly headed past Keiren Westwood in the Owls' goal. It was a classy finish.

Wednesday pushed with urgency for an equaliser and they should've been awarded a penalty when Jacob Murphy skipped by his marker before being upended. Instead, the referee gave free-kick just inches outside of the box. Garry Monk and his players were fuming as the initial foul was clearly inside the white-line.

Although nothing came of the consequent free-kick, it was Murphy who provided Adam Reach with a chance in the final minute of injury-time but he blazed his shot way over the bar. The Owls were left ruing decent chances in both halves of the tie.

This defeat saw Sheffield Wednesday slip to ninth in the league table and next up was an important home tie with Wigan Athletic.

**League position:** 9th

**Hull City starting eleven:** Long, Lichaj, Burke, de Wijs, Fleming, Stewart, Bowen, Honeyman (Batty 77'), Irvine, Grosicki (Bowler 87'), Magennis (Eaves 66').

**Sheffield Wednesday starting eleven:** Westwood, Odubajo, Iorfa, Börner, Palmer, Reach, Hutchinson (Lee 78'), Bannan, Harris (Murphy 59'), Winnall (Rhodes 68'), Nuhiu.

## 3pm Saturday 5th October, Hillsborough (Attendance: 22,753)

### Sheffield Wednesday 1-0 Wigan Athletic (Luongo 57')

Massimo Luongo's second-half strike guaranteed the points and kept the Owls in the play-off hunt.

Wednesday came closest to scoring in the first-half when a curling Barry Bannan effort bounced back off the frame from twenty-yards.

The only goal of the game came in the second period courtesy of an Adam Reach cut-back which found Luongo; he then placed the ball neatly beyond David Marshall in the Lactics net. This was the Australian's first goal for the club on what was his maiden league appearance in the starting eleven.

The visitors also had a handful of opportunities to score but Westwood was on hand to keep Wigan at bay. One save in particular from a Kieffer Moore header was tipped onto the bar spectacularly by the Republic of Ireland international.

Likewise to the previous contest with Hull City, the officiating was in the spotlight once again. Steven Fletcher volleyed home an obstructed Adam Reach shot but the goal was ruled out for offside. Replays suggested that Fletcher was near enough in line with the last two Wigan defenders, yet the Owls managed to see out the game and this win saw them climb to eighth in the table.

Sheffield Wednesday had won six of their last seven league encounters versus Wigan and remarkably, only three points separated first to ninth in the Championship standings.

Succeeding this win, Fernando Forestieri had served his six match suspension and was eligible to return against Cardiff City in two-weeks time. Bring it on!

**League position:** 8th

**Sheffield Wednesday starting eleven:** Westwood, Odubajo, Iorfa, Börner, Palmer, Pelupessy, Reach (Murphy 80'), Luongo (Lee 75'), Bannan, Harris, Fletcher (Nuhiu 89').

**Wigan Athletic starting eleven:** Marshall, Byrne, Dunkley, Mulgrew, Robinson, Williams, Morsy, Massey (Pilkington 64'), Windass, Lowe (Gelhardt 78'), Garner (Moore 64').

**7.45pm Friday 18th October, Cardiff City Stadium (Attendance: 22,486)**

**Cardiff City 1-1 Sheffield Wednesday** (Börner 19', Tomlin 87')

Lee Tomlin's late but controversial free-kick rescued a point for the Bluebirds which cancelled out Julian Börner's opener for the Owls.

Wednesday were on top from the off and it was Börner who gave the Owls an early advantage. His guided side-foot effort hit the back of the net when he essentially finished off a Kadeem Harris strike from nineteen-yards.

Harris, who was facing his former club did rattle the cross bar with a well-executed free-kick and was very unlucky not to score. Regardless of numerous half chances, the Owls were unable to double their lead before half-time.

After sixty-minutes, Wednesday were naive and allowed Cardiff City to push forward. The hosts hit the post and had a penalty shout waved away as they searched for an equaliser. It was then in the eighty-seventh-minute when substitute Lee Tomlin found the net with a great free-kick that dipped into the corner of Dawson's goal.

Although the original set-piece probably shouldn't have been awarded, questions were raised over the officiating for the third Wednesday fixture in a row. Aiden Flint was believed to be interfering with play when he stood in an offside position and was doing star-jumps in Dawson's line of sight. Still, the goal was allowed to stand at the enragement of the Owls players and management staff.

Cardiff's controversial goal was the main talking point at full-time and Garry Monk was made to live with another poor game changing decision. Wednesday had to make the long journey home from Wales with just a point.

This result also ensured that the Owls' bad luck was sustained in Wales having not won there in twelve league outings. Their last victory at Cardiff was in 2007.

**League position:** 8th

**Cardiff City starting eleven:** Etheridge, Peltier, Morrison, Flint, Bennett, Bacuna (Ward 34'), Pack, Ralls, Mendez-Laing (Whyte 76'), Glatzel (Tomlin 76'), Murphy.

**Sheffield Wednesday starting eleven:** Dawson, Palmer, Iorfa, Börner, Fox, Hutchinson, Reach, Luongo, Bannan (Nuhiu 73'), Harris (Murphy 79'), Fletcher.

**7.45pm Tuesday 22<sup>nd</sup> October, Hillsborough (Attendance: 22,460)**

**Sheffield Wednesday 1-0 Stoke City** (Luongo 43')

A Massimo Luongo strike was enough to keep up the Owls' fantastic win record on Tuesdays at Hillsborough.

It soon became apparent that luck wasn't on the visitor's side when they lost two players through injury in the opening thirty-minutes.

The home side did look more likely to score and they

had to wait until the forty-third-minute to do so. Massimo Luongo's determination saw him benefit from a Steven Fletcher knock down, the Australian central-midfielder then powered past Stoke City's last man before slotting home.

The Potters did improve in the second-half and came closest to scoring when Lee Gregory's header was saved at point-blank-range by Cameron Dawson.

In a game that was scrappy overall, Sheffield Wednesday managed to hold on for the win despite being under the cosh in the final thirty-minutes. There was also an additional seven-minutes of added-time that Garry Monk's side had to see pass.

The Owls had now won four fixtures in a row when playing at home on a Tuesday and extraordinarily had only lost only twice in their last twenty-three matches on this day at S6. Additionally, Wednesday were now unbeaten in seven league ties versus Stoke City since their last defeat in 2005.

Ahead of more mid-week fixtures, this victory saw Wednesday on the tails of the top two. An interesting contest against the promotion favourites now awaited on Saturday...

**League position:** 3rd

**Sheffield Wednesday starting eleven:** Dawson, Palmer, Iorfa, Börner, Fox, Hutchinson, Reach, Luongo (Lee 54'), Bannan, Harris (Forestieri 74'), Fletcher (Nuhiu 81').

**Stoke City starting eleven:** Federici, Edwards, Carter-Vickers (Lindsay 27'), Batth, Ward, Etebo (Duffy 21'), Ndiaye, Allen, Clucas, Campbell (Hogan 69'), Gregory.

## 12.30pm Saturday 26<sup>th</sup> October, Hillsborough (Attendance: 27,516)

### Sheffield Wednesday 0-0 Leeds United

Sheffield Wednesday and Leeds United both missed the opportunity to sit top of the table after this goalless draw at Hillsborough.

In a game that saw Garry Monk face one of his former clubs, the tie looked full of goals as both sides created decent chances.

Patrick Bamford came closest for the visitors on the stroke of half-time when his directed header was superbly saved by Keiren Westwood with his fingertips. This save was one for the cameras and was undoubtedly the best save of the campaign so far.

In the second-half, Steven Fletcher almost notched the opening goal with a thunderous effort from outside the area; the ball rattled the bar and then bounced clear off the back of Casilla in the Leeds United sticks. Soon after, Ezgjan Alioski almost stole the victory for Leeds but his guided header came back off the post.

In a game that was deserving of a winner, Atdhe Nuhiu

had a header comfortably saved and Kadeem Harris saw his curling shot tipped over. Morgan Fox had to make a goal-line clearance at the other end from a Jack Harrison strike.

When the final whistle blew, this was the first time Sheffield Wednesday and Leeds United had drawn nil-nil since April 1969. This goalless draw also ensured that no side had kept as many clean sheets in the 2019 calendar year than the Owls, with sixteen in total at this stage.

Wednesday were now unbeaten in four league fixtures.

**League position:** 5th

**Sheffield Wednesday starting eleven:** Westwood, Palmer, Iorfa, Hutchinson, Fox, Reach, Pelupessy (Lee 84'), Bannan, Harris, Nuhiu (Forestieri 86'), Fletcher.

**Leeds United starting eleven:** Casilla, Ayling, White, Berardi, Dallas, Phillips, Klich, Alioski, Helder Costa (Cooper 76'), Bamford (Nketiah 45'), Harrison.

**3pm Saturday 2$^{nd}$ November, Ewood Park (Attendance: 14,147)**

**Blackburn Rovers 2-1 Sheffield Wednesday** (Murphy 83', Adarabioyo 88', Buckley 90+1')

Blackburn Rovers clinched the win by scoring two quick-fire goals at the death only a few minutes after the Owls had taken the lead.

In a tie that was pretty dire until midway through the second-half, it was substitute Jacob Murphy who put Wednesday ahead with only seven-minutes of normal time remaining. Steven Fletcher's close range pivoting shot hit the bar only for Murphy to head in the rebound from one-yard.

Blackburn drew level five-minutes later when a drifted free-kick found the head of Tosin Adarabioyo and the ball looped over Keiren Westwood. Soon after, in what was an extraordinary finale, Rovers were ahead. Substitute John Buckley struck his first senior goal when a deflected shot hit the net from twenty-yards.

The Owls almost equalised in the ninety-fourth-minute when Fernando Forestieri's shot came back off the post, then Sam Hutchinson's follow-up somehow dashed across the face of goal with Fletcher and Nuhiu loitering.

The travelling Wednesday faithful were left exasperated when the whistle blew. This loss was a tough pill to swallow.

**League position:** 7th

**Blackburn Rovers starting eleven:** Walton, Bennett, Nyambe, Adarabioyo, Williams, Travis, Downing (Buckley 87'), Holtby (Rothwell 67'), Dack, Armstrong, Gallagher (Graham 64').

**Sheffield Wednesday starting eleven:** Westwood, Palmer, Iorfa, Börner, Fox, Hutchinson, Reach (Murphy 70'), Lee, Pelupessy (Forestieri 61'), Harris (Nuhiu 77'), Fletcher.


**3pm Saturday 9th November, Hillsborough (Attendance: 23,073)**

**Sheffield Wednesday 2-2 Swansea City** (Ayew 32', Forestieri 81', Fox 90+1', Wilmot 90+4')

Sheffield Wednesday once again failed to see out the win in this entertaining score draw at Hillsborough.

In what was the last fixture in the Championship before the international break, the Owls started brightly and should've taken the lead as they conjured up numerous chances early on; Steven Fletcher came closest when his header crashed against the post.

Despite Wednesday's attacking threat it was the Swans who scored first against the run of play. Succeeding a corner, Andre Ayew pounced on a defensive mix-up to poke home from six-yards.

The Owls almost netted in the second-half but Jacob Murphy's shot smashed the post after Woodman had fumbled a Nuhiu header.

Sheffield Wednesday's equaliser finally arrived when Adam Reach drove forward and powered a shot towards goal but his initial strike was parried. Kieran Lee was the man on hand to cut-back before the onrushing Fernando Forestieri applied the simple finish.

In injury-time, Morgan Fox looked a likely hero when he tried his luck with a half-volley and the ball hit the roof of the Swansea net; the Wednesday players began to rejoice.

Just when the home side thought they had bagged all three points, the visitors levelled through a Ben Wilmot header in the ninety-fourth-minute. The majority of the Owls defence were in no man's land and they only had themselves to blame.

This tie left the fans with mixed emotions at full-time, particularly because the Owls had failed to put the fixture to bed for the second consecutive game in a row. In many ways this draw felt like a loss.

On a positive note, Sheffield Wednesday had still only lost one league game against Swansea City at Hillsborough in their previous fifteen head-to-heads. The Owls now had a two-week break to endure.

**League position:** 8th

**Sheffield Wednesday starting eleven:** Westwood, Palmer, Iorfa, Lees, Fox, Murphy (Reach 76'), Lee, Bannan, Harris (Rhodes 83'), Nuhiu (Forestieri 66'), Fletcher.

**Swansea City starting eleven:** Woodman, Naughton, Wilmot, van der Hoorn, Bidwell, Byers, Grimes, Dyer (Roberts 77'), Celina (Fulton 83'), Routledge (Surridge 87'), Ayew.

## Looming Misconduct Charges

On Thursday the 14th November, Sheffield Wednesday football club were charged with misconduct following the sale of Hillsborough stadium. These alleged breaches were in relation to the Chairman selling the Owls' ground to himself in an attempt to avoid particular profit and sustainability spending rules.

While Dejphon Chansiri had only made use of a loop hole in which other clubs had pursued, the English Football League had reviewed the sale and concluded that there was sufficient evidence to justify sanctions. These possible punishments included point's deductions, financial consequences, further embargoes or even the possibility of eviction from the football league.

Sheffield Wednesday had the opportunity to stand firm, defend and deny the misconduct charges put to them if they could provide evidence of a fair transaction.

Financial fair play and the rules within them remained a hot topic of discussion at S6 since the arrival of wealthy businessman Chansiri in 2015. Championship teams are only allowed to record a loss of £39 million over a three year period, hence the sale of Hillsborough stadium. This ensured Sheffield Wednesday made a pre-tax profit in 2017/18. Even so, the major issue raised by the English Football League appeared to be over the timing of the business deal.

These potential misconduct charges would now play a huge role in determining the outcome of the 2019/20 campaign both on and off the field. The remainder of the season would become a very anxious period. Still, the Owls were not the first Championship club to sell their own stadium; similar situations also took place Aston Villa, Derby County and Reading, with the English Football League continuing to analyse these trades.

As the ruckus between both parties remained constant over time, the English Football League continued to insist they had sufficient proof to charge Sheffield Wednesday. On the other hand, the Owls persisted in fighting these charges by proceeding with the arbitrators to contest and hopefully resolve the matter sooner rather than later.

As the months passed by and still without any conclusion to the dispute, it appeared as though these looming misconduct charges would drag on until the seasons end. Nevertheless, the inevitable outcome had to arrive, eventually.

For the time being the Owls had to turn their attentions to matters on the field and next up was a difficult trip the league leaders…

## The 2019/20 Campaign Continued…

### 3pm Saturday 23rd November, The Hawthorns (Attendance: 25,566)

**West Bromwich Albion 2-1 Sheffield Wednesday** (Robson-Kanu 10', Fletcher Penalty 58', Austin Penalty 88', Palmer Sent Off 90+2')

The Owls suffered another defeat on the road after a late Charlie Austin penalty ensured West Brom remained at the top of the table.

Wednesday found themselves behind just ten-minutes into the fixture when a defence splitting pass saw Robson-Kanu run through on goal, he then placed the ball beyond the onrushing Keiren Westwood.

In a game that saw both sides creating good chances, Sheffield Wednesday managed to pull level in the second-half when Kieran Lee dispossessed Krovinovic; as a result, Lee was pulled down in the area. Steven Fletcher stepped up and nervelessly slotted the penalty straight down the centre of the goal.

As both sides continued to push for the winner, Morgan Fox almost gave Wednesday the lead but his glancing strike smashed the bar and went over. Substitute Charlie Austin then had a header hit the post for the home side. The contest really could've gone either way.

With only minutes remaining in the tie, somewhat of a nothing ball was sent over the top of the Owls defence. This led to a miscommunication between goalkeeper and right-back, only for Westwood to concede a cruel penalty kick. Austin made no mistake from the spot to secure maximum points for his side.

To make matters worse, Liam Palmer was sent off in injury-time because of a uncharacteristic but reckless challenge; this was Palmer's first dismissal in his Owls career and he would now serve a three match suspension.

This result made certain that Sheffield Wednesday had still not beaten any side in the top-half of the division so far this season.

**League position:** 9th

**West Bromwich Albion starting eleven:** Johnstone, Furlong, Bartley, Hegazi (Barry 74'), Townsend, Krovinovic (Brunt 81'), Ajayi, Phillips, Pereira, Diangana, Robson-Kanu (Austin 75').

**Sheffield Wednesday starting eleven:** Westwood, Palmer, Iorfa, Börner, Fox, Hutchinson (Nuhiu 89'), Murphy, Lee (Luongo 70'), Bannan, Harris (Reach 60'), Fletcher.

**7.45pm Wednesday 27<sup>th</sup> November, Hillsborough (Attendance: 22,059)**

**Sheffield Wednesday 1 -1 Birmingham City** (Giminez 48', Harris 81')

Kadeem Harris rescued a point for the Owls in the contest that saw Garry Monk face his former club for the first time since his departure.

Tensions were high before kick-off due to Garry Monk's pre-match remarks towards the Blues' chief Pep Clotet. Both managers had previously worked together at Birmingham City during the 2018/19 term and Monk didn't hide the fact he was left irritated with Pep. As a result, Monk never shook Clotet's hand in the dugout prior to kick-off.

With the match under-way, Wednesday almost opened the scoring when Moses Odubajo cut inside and released a thunder-bolt of a shot from twenty-five yards but his effort rattled the bar.

Just minutes into the second-half and against the run of play, it was the travelling side who took the lead. Jeremie Bela drifted a low cross into the area before Alvaro Giminez neatly turned the ball home from close range.

With less than ten-minutes left on the clock, Sheffield Wednesday deservedly found an equaliser thanks to Kadeem Harris. The pacey winger pushed forward on the right and after a short mazy run he let loose from twenty-yards, his effort was too precise for Trueman in the sticks and Harris ran off to celebrate.

With the tie now level it was the Owls who had the momentum, they were unlucky not to nick the win late on when Massimo Luongo's header was cleared off the line. Both sides had to make do with a point in the end.

This result kept Garry Monk's unbeaten league record at Hillsborough intact, although Wednesday had not won in their previous five league outings.

**League position:** 10th

**Sheffield Wednesday starting eleven:** Dawson, Odubajo, Iorfa, Börner (Lees 45'), Fox, Reach (Nuhiu 67'), Lee (Forestieri 56'), Bannan, Luongo, Harris, Fletcher.

**Birmingham City starting eleven:** Trueman, Colin, Roberts, Clarke-Salter, Pedersen, Crowley, Sunjic, Bellingham (Davis 82'), Villalba Rodrigo, Bela (Montero 70'), Giminez (Jutkiewicz 66').

**12.30pm Saturday 30th November, The Valley (Attendance: 18,338)**

**Charlton Athletic 1-3 Sheffield Wednesday** (Fletcher 17', Bonne 26', Fletcher Penalty 80', Nuhiu 90+4')

A Steven Fletcher brace guaranteed Wednesday the win at the anguish of the new on-looking Charlton Athletic owners.

The first goal of the game came when Barry Bannan distributed a delightful ball into the area; Fletcher was there to finish with a powerful trademark header.

The Owls should've doubled their lead midway through the second-half but Fernando Forestieri was the culprit of a glaring miss from six-yards.

Minutes later, the score was level when Alfie Doughty found enough space to cross the from the left; the ball dropped to Macauley Bonne whose attempt deflected off Tom Lees and went in off the post.

In spite of the equaliser it was Wednesday who remained on top throughout the tie. The Owls managed to take the lead ten-minutes from time when Steven Fletcher scored his second of the game. Jacob Murphy was toppled over on the right before the Scottish front-man slid the penalty beyond Phillips in the Addicks net.

With the three points in sight, Atdhe Nuhiu sealed the victory with his third goal of the campaign. Adam Reach found the unmarked Kosovon international with a delicate cross into the box before he directed his header into the roof of the Charlton net. Once again, that was another goal for Atdhe in added-time.

Sheffield Wednesday were worthy of their win and they were hopeful that this victory was a turning point after their bad run of form. The Owls were now just two points behind Preston North-End who occupied the final play-off spot.

**League position:** 9th

**Charlton Athletic starting eleven:** Phillips, Matthews, Lockyer, Sarr, Doughty, Oshilaja, Pratley, Morgan (Vennings 61'), Oztumer (Davison 81'), Bonne, Leko.

**Sheffield Wednesday starting eleven:** Dawson, Odubajo, Iorfa, Lees, Fox, Harris (Reach 81'), Hutchinson (Luongo 77'), Bannan, Forestieri (Murphy 45'), Fletcher, Nuhiu.

**3pm Saturday 7$^{th}$ December, Hillsborough (Attendance: 22,475)**

**Sheffield Wednesday 2-1 Brentford** (Mbeumo 29', Fletcher Penalty 69', Fletcher 73')

Sheffield Wednesday moved into the play-off places after reversing a one-nil deficit thanks to a Steven Fletcher double in the second-half.

It was Brentford who took the lead just before the half-hour mark. Josh Dasilva whipped in a corner and found the head of Bryan Mbeumo who scored from close range. That wasn't the first time that the Owls had been vulnerable from set-pieces this season.

After half-time and with Wednesday on the ascendancy, they were awarded a spot-kick when Bees defender Rico Henry handled in the area. Steven Fletcher did the rest as he converted the ball down the centre of the goal.

The contest was suddenly overturned four-minutes later and it was that man again, Fletcher. Following a cross from Kadeem Harris, the six-foot-one-inch striker controlled the ball and smashed his left-foot shot past the helpless David Raya.

The Scottish front-man enjoyed that one and was consequently booked for the removal of his blue and white jersey. That was his tenth goal of the season.

At full-time, the Owls were unbeaten in seven league fixtures at home and had finally beat a side in the top half of the table for the first time this season.

**League position:** 6th

**Sheffield Wednesday starting eleven:** Dawson, Odubajo, Iorfa, Lees, Fox, Murphy (Reach 63'), Hutchinson (Luongo 78'), Bannan, Harris, Nuhiu (Rhodes 45'), Fletcher.

**Brentford starting eleven:** Raya, Rasmussen, Jeanvier, Pinnock, Henry, Mokotjo (Jensen 71'), Norgaard, Dasilva, Mbeumo, Watkins, Benrahma.

**7.45pm Wednesday 11ᵗʰ December, Pride Park (Attendance: 26,203)**

**Derby County 1-1 Sheffield Wednesday** (Fletcher 23', Martin Penalty 82', Odubajo Sent Off 90')

A late Derby County penalty ensured Sheffield Wednesday slipped out of the play-off places as the points were shared at Pride Park.

During a dominant first-half display, the Owls made the breakthrough when Barry Bannan got hold of a loose ball and played a quick pass to his associate Steven Fletcher. From twenty-yards the Wednesday number nine curled a precise first-time shot beyond Ben Hamer in the Rams' goal. That was his fifth goal in his previous three outings.

Regardless of Sheffield Wednesday's earlier pressure the home side drew level thanks to a contentious penalty decision with less than ten-minutes remaining. The referee pointed to the spot when Moses Odubajo and Jack Marriott tangled inside the area and fell to the turf.

After the Owls players had objected to the suspicious decision, Chris Martin successfully slammed home from twelve-yards.

Things soon went from bad to worse for the Wednesday right-back when he was shown a second yellow for obstructing Scott Malone. Off he went down the tunnel. When it arrived the final whistle came as a relief to both sides.

In a contest that the Owls should've won during the ninety, they had still not won at Pride Park in their previous twelve attempts in all competitions. The Derby County curse continued.

**League position:** 8th

**Derby County starting eleven:** Hamer, Bogle, Davies, Forsyth, Malone, Knight (Marriott 68'), Evans, Whittaker (Waghorn 68'), Holmes, Lawrence, Martin.

**Sheffield Wednesday starting eleven:** Dawson, Odubajo, Iorfa, Lees, Fox, Reach, Hutchinson, Bannan, Harris (Murphy 61'), Rhodes (Nuhiu 72'), Fletcher (Luongo 79').

**3pm Saturday 14th December, City Ground (Attendance: 28,002)**

**Nottingham Forest 0-4 Sheffield Wednesday** (Rhodes 9', Rhodes 13', Rhodes 37', Fletcher 45+3')

Jordan Rhodes scored a perfect hat-trick in the first-half as the Owls ran riot at the City Ground.

Sheffield Wednesday got off to a flying start and were two-nil up within the first fifteen-minutes of the tie. Jordan Rhodes, who had not scored in the league April 2018 drilled home a left-foot shot as the ball fell to him inside of the Forest area.

Within minutes, the away side doubled their advantage when Adam Reach picked out Rhodes in the box with an exquisite delivery from the right. The Owls number six comfortably powered his header past the helpless keeper. Two-nil!

Succeeding a corner, the travelling Wednesday faithful couldn't believe their eyes when Jordan Rhodes scored his third goal of the game with an overhead kick with his right-foot. Wow!

The previously overlooked Owls forward was taking home the match ball and there was still fifty-minutes left to play. That was the first time in five-years and nine-months that the Scottish striker had scored three goals in a fixture.

Sheffield Wednesday were relentless and added a fourth during first-half injury-time. Following a corner, the ball fell loose and Steven Fletcher was there to prod home. The Owls' fans were ecstatic.

Having done all of the hard work during the opening forty-five-minutes, Wednesday successfully soaked up all the pressure during the second-half to win at ease.

This was a huge win for the Owls having almost mirrored Nottingham Forest in the table all season. Sheffield Wednesday had won nine of their previous ten league fixtures versus Forest, losing only once.

**League position:** 5th

**Nottingham Forest starting eleven:** Samba, Cash, Dawson, Worrall, Robinson, Yates, Watson, Carvalho, Silva,

Ameobi, Grabban.

**Sheffield Wednesday starting eleven:** Dawson, Palmer, Iorfa, Lees (Börner 78'), Fox, Reach, Luongo, Bannan, Harris, Rhodes (Winnall 87'), Fletcher (Nuhiu 81').

**12pm Sunday 22nd December, Hillsborough (Attendance: 23,180)**

**Sheffield Wednesday 1-0 Bristol City (**Bannan Penalty 85')

A Barry Bannan spot-kick saw the Owls climb to third at the halfway stage of the season.

The travelling side should've found themselves in front after only fifteen-seconds but Callum O'Dowda's strike went glaringly wide.

Wednesday had a couple of chances that fell to Liam Palmer and Adam Reach in the first-half but they both failed to hit the net. The game was scoreless at half-time.

Bristol City went close as the sides returned for the second period, Weimann's header had Cameron Dawson beaten but Palmer was in the right place at the right time to make a goal-line clearance.

Having already had a couple of penalty shouts turned down, the referee pointed to the spot with only five-minutes of normal time remaining when Atdhe Nuhiu hit the deck. Even though the spot-kick decision looked a little soft soft, Barry Bannan stepped up and applied a subtle finish. Wednesday had got the win that they deserved.

When the final whistle blew, the Owls were unbeaten in six league contests and had beaten Bristol City three times in a row for the first time since 1971. This win also ensured Wednesday would be sat third in the table on Christmas day.

**League position:** 3rd

**Sheffield Wednesday starting eleven:** Dawson, Palmer, Iorfa, Lees, Fox (Börner 30'), Reach, Luongo (Pelupessy 90'), Bannan, Harris, Rhodes (Winnall 76'), Nuhiu.

**Bristol City starting eleven:** Bentley, Kalas, Williams, Moore, Hunt (Eliasson 61'), Brownhill, Smith, O'Dowda, Rowe (Semenyo 86'), Weimann (Palmer 61'), Diedhiou.

**3pm Thursday 26<sup>th</sup> December, bet365 Stadium (Attendance: 25,359)**

**Stoke City 3-2 Sheffield Wednesday** (McClean 11', Fox 67', Lees 74', Campbell 90+3', Vokes 90+7')

Stoke City scored two goals in added-time to end Sheffield Wednesday's successful run of six league fixtures without a loss.

The Potters took an early lead when James McClean pounced on Joe Allen's shot to tap-in on the goal-line. Remarkably, this was the first goal Sheffield Wednesday had conceded on Boxing Day in eight-years.

Just after the half-hour mark, the Owls almost equalised when Adam Reach headed against the post from a fizzing Harris cross.

Then with their first shot on target and against the run of play, Wednesday drew level in the second-half when Morgan Fox scored with the flick of his back-heel at the near post from a Barry Bannan corner.

It was just eight-minutes later when the Owls hit the net again. Bannan found Winnall's head but the ball was tipped onto the bar by Jack Butland; Tom Lees was the quickest to react and he gave Wednesday the advantage.

Sheffield Wednesday then fell apart in injury-time. The collapse began when Tyrese Campbell powered his shot into the roof of Dawson's net to level the contest.

Sam Vokes then sealed the victory for the Potters in the ninety-seventh-minute when he scrambled his effort over the Owls' goal-line from six-yards.

Incredibly, this was Cameron Dawson's first loss in an Owls jersey in 2019. This defeat also confirmed that conceding goals at the death was still a common trend; Wednesday were miles off the pace in this tie and in many ways their performance warranted a defeat.

**League position:** 4th

**Stoke City starting eleven:** Butland, Smith, Batth, Shawcross, Ward (Vokes 78'), Allen, Cousins, Clucas, Ince, Gregory (Campbell 73'), McClean.

**Sheffield Wednesday starting eleven:** Dawson, Palmer, Iorfa, Lees, Fox, Reach, Luongo (Hutchinson 57'), Bannan, Harris, Rhodes (Winnall 59'), Nuhiu (Murphy 65').

**3pm Sunday 29<sup>th</sup> December, Hillsborough (Attendance: 25,385)**

**Sheffield Wednesday 1-2 Cardiff City** (Glatzel 5', Hoilett 8', Lees 18')

Garry Monk suffered his first league defeat at Hillsborough in what was Sheffield Wednesday's final fixture of 2019.

It was the Bluebirds who found the net with their first attack of the tie, Robert Glatzel brought the ball under control and drilled his shot into the Wednesday goal.

It was just three-minutes later when the away side doubled their lead. Lee Tomlin found space on the right and crossed the ball into the path of the unmarked Junior Hoilett, who precisely slammed the ball home. It was a terrible start for the Owls.

Sheffield Wednesday pulled a goal back when Tom Lees scored a header at the back post from a Barry Bannan corner. That was the captain's second goal in as many games. Game on!

Despite the possession and shot statistics suggesting that Wednesday were the most penetrative side, they never managed to overcome their downfall in the early stages of the tie. Atdhe Nuhiu did burst through on goal in the ninety-seventh-minute but his effort went agonisingly wide.

This was the first time the Owls had lost against Cardiff City since 2015.

**League position:** 6th

**Sheffield Wednesday starting eleven:** Dawson, Palmer (Börner 63') Iorfa (Rhodes 58'), Lees, Fox, Hutchinson, Bannan, Murphy (Nuhiu 80'), Reach, Harris, Winnall.

**Cardiff City starting eleven:** Etheridge, Richards, Flint, Nelson, Bennett (Vaulks 36'), Bacuna, Pack, Mendez-Laing (Bamba 42'), Tomlin (Paterson 83'), Hoilett, Glatzel.

# ENTERING A NEW DECADE

*Make Or Break?*

With two losses on the bounce, the Owls still found themselves in the final play-off spot at the turn of the new year. If Sheffield Wednesday were going to be successful this season, each of the remaining twenty-one league games would be significant. The fixtures would come thick and fast so Garry Monk knew that consistency would be key.

With the January transfer window now open for the next thirty-one-days, it was possible that the Owls had some room to manoeuvre. It was make or break time.

Next up in the league was a very winnable home tie to Hull City on New Years Day.

# The 2019/20 Campaign Continued…

### 3pm Wednesday 1st January, Hillsborough (Attendance: 24,842)

### Sheffield Wednesday 0-1 Hull City (Bowen 61')

Sheffield Wednesday entered the new decade with a disappointing loss to Hull and subsequently fell out of the top six in the league standings.

The travelling side squandered the opportunity to take an early lead when Matthew Pennington's attempt from close range somehow went wide of the post.

Regardless of the Owls' lack lustre performance they were still guilty of wasted chances during the ninety. Kadeem Harris had an effort cleared off the line, Atdhe Nuhiu headed straight into the hands of the City keeper and Steven Fletcher had a scrappy shot bounce clear off the upright.

The Owls were made to pay just after the hour when Jarrod Bowen condemned Wednesday to another defeat. George Honeyman fired a cross towards the penalty spot before the talisman instinctively slotted his half-volley into the Wednesday net.

This was the first time the Owls had suffered a third successive league defeat since November 2018 and it was safe to say that the festive period had been one to forget.

**League position:** 8th

**Sheffield Wednesday starting eleven:** Dawson, Iorfa, Lees, Börner, Fox, Reach (Murphy 64'), Hutchinson, Bannan, Harris, Nuhiu (Fletcher 45'), Winnall (Rhodes 60').

**Hull City starting eleven:** Long, Pennington, Burke, de Wijs, Lichaj, Irvine, Batty, Bowen, Honeyman (Da Silva Lopes 72'), Grosicki (Lewis-Potter 79'), Eaves (Bowler 80').

**FA Cup Round Three - 3.01pm Saturday 4th January, The Amex (Attendance: 20,349)**

**Brighton and Hove Albion 0-1 Sheffield Wednesday** (Reach 65')

Sheffield Wednesday progressed into the FA Cup fourth round after seeing off Brighton and Hove Albion of the Premier League.

Prior to kick-off there was a surprise name in the starting eleven, teenager Osaze Urhoghide was all set to make his senior debut at right-back and he didn't disappoint.

Both sides created a couple of chances during the opening forty-five-minutes but it was Steven Fletcher who came closest on the stroke of half-time. He smashed a volley towards goal and David Button had to produce a wonderful agile save to keep the thirty-two-year-old at bay.

The Owls started the second-half brightly and managed to get their noses in front with a well worked free-kick. Winnall and Murphy confused the Brighton wall with a quick training ground routine before Reach hit the shot low and hard, subsequently the ball deflected into the net and the travelling faithful went wild.

The Owls held on. Adam Reach's strike turned out to be the only goal of the game and that confirmed a trip to QPR in the FA Cup fourth round.

This was the first time that the Owls had beaten Premier League opponents in the FA Cup since the 1992/93 campaign having not won in their previous twenty attempts.

The only headache that Garry Monk suffered following this tie was the injury to Steven Fletcher. One of Sheffield Wednesday's most influential players so far this term was set to face up to three-months on the side-lines. It was a huge setback.

**Brighton and Hove Albion starting eleven:** Button, Duffy, Balogun (Connolly 45'), Webster, Bong (Bernardo 71'), Alzate, Bissouma (Jahanbakhsh 63'), Stephens, Schelotto, Grob, Maupay.

**Sheffield Wednesday starting eleven:** Dawson, Fox, Urhoghide, Börner, Iorfa, Lee, Reach (Lees 90'), Pelupessy, Luongo, Murphy (Harris 71'), Fletcher (Winnall 55').

**3pm Saturday 11<sup>th</sup> January, Elland Road (Attendance: 36,422)**

**Leeds United 0-2 Sheffield Wednesday** (Murphy 87', Nuhiu 90+4')

Sheffield Wednesday upset their promotion chasing Yorkshire rivals with two goals at the death.

Leeds United had their fair share of possession during the opening forty-five-minutes but the Owls managed to remain compact. The tie was goalless at halfway stage.

Wednesday began the second-half on the front foot and should've taken the lead in the fifty-fourth-minute. The ball fell to Sam Winnall in the area but he blazed over from six-yards, it was a hands on head moment for the Owls number eleven.

The game opened up but it was Wednesday who found the net with only a few minutes of normal time remaining. Substitute Atdhe Nuhiu played a neat pass to Jacob Murphy on the right; he carried the ball forward, pulled the trigger and blasted beyond Casilla from a tight angle. One-nil!

In added-time, after a delightful Barry Bannan through ball, Adam Reach drove a pin-point cross into the path of Nuhiu from the left. Calm as you like the mountainous forward shot into the top left corner of the goal to put the game to bed. Once again, Nuhiu had managed to bag another goal in added-time. His tally was now up to four for the season.

As well as the win, this was the first time Sheffield Wednesday had managed to keep a clean sheet at Elland Road in the league since 1996. Likewise to the trips to Middlesbrough and Nottingham Forest, this victory was one of the highlights of the season so far.

**League position:** 6th

**Leeds United starting eleven:** Casilla, Ayling, White, Cooper, Douglas (Alioski 56'), Phillips, Helder Costa (Stevens 75'), Dallas, Klich (Hernandez 66'), Harrison, Bamford.

**Sheffield Wednesday starting eleven:** Dawson, Urhoghide (Hutchinson 85'), Iorfa, Börner, Fox, Luongo (Pelupessy 77'), Lee, Reach, Bannan, Murphy, Winnall (Nuhiu 69').


**3pm Saturday 18<sup>th</sup> January, Hillsborough (Attendance: 23,504)**

**Sheffield Wednesday 0-5 Blackburn Rovers** (Holty 19', Luongo Sent Off 23', Holtby 45+1', Dawson Own Goal 36', Lenihan 48', Gallagher 90+2')

Sheffield Wednesday were left red faced as Blackburn Rovers thumped five past Garry Monk's side.

Rovers scored their first when Adam Armstrong cut the ball back after his initial shot was parried by Dawson;

Lewis Holtby was there to apply the simple finish.

Within five-minutes of conceding, Wednesday were down to ten men when Massimo Luongo embarked on a fifty-fifty challenge with Lewis Travis. Without hesitation the referee flashed a red-card, it looked a yellow-card at best and the boos began to ring around Hillsborough. Luongo had barely touched the Rovers defender.

Things only got worse in the thirty-sixth-minute when Lewis Travis' effort was tipped onto the woodwork by Cameron Dawson, the ball then hit Dawson on the back of the head and went over the goal-line.

Sheffield Wednesday's afternoon soon turned into a disaster when Blackburn found a third on the stroke of half-time. Lewis Holtby notched his second goal of the game when he tapped in from six-yards after Adam Armstrong had torn through Wednesday's defence.

There was no way back. Irrespective of the harsh sending off the Owls were second best all over the park.

The away side were at it again and added a fourth just minutes into the second-half. Following a quick corner, Downing swung in a cross before Lenihan volleyed home. Enough was enough for some Wednesdayites as many headed for the exit if they hadn't already done so.

The nightmare wasn't over just yet, Sam Gallagher wrapped things up for Rovers in injury-time when he beat the offside trap and drilled his shot past Dawson.

When the final whistle blew, Sheffield Wednesday had

lost three consecutive home games in a row. It was a diabolical showing, this result was a gentle reminder that the Owls had been very inconsistent since November. It was time to go back to the drawing board.

Post-match, Sheffield Wednesday appealed the red card of Massimo Luongo and his sending off was rescinded just a few days later. Justice had been served.

**League position:** 10th

**Sheffield Wednesday starting eleven:** Dawson, Urhoghide (Lees 45'), Iorfa, Börner, Fox, Lee (Hutchinson 45'), Murphy, Luongo, Bannan, Reach, Winnall (Nuhiu 37').

**Blackburn Rovers starting eleven:** Walton, Nyambe, Lenihan, Adarabioyo, Bell, Travis (Davenport 73'), Downing, Rothwell (Rankin-Costello 59'), Holtby, Armstrong (Brereton 87'), Gallagher.

**FA Cup Round Four - 8pm Friday 24th January, Kiyan Prince Foundation Stadium (Attendance: 11,871)**

**Queens Park Rangers 1-2 Sheffield Wednesday** (Fox 43', Winnall 90+1', Wells 90+3')

Sheffield Wednesday triumphed against one of their Championship rivals to reach the last sixteen of the FA Cup.

Neither side were able to capitalise on half chances until the Owls got their noses in front just before half-time. Sam Hutchinson quickly distributed a throw-in into the path of Morgan Fox who prodded his shot past Lumley. The Rangers keeper probably should've saved Fox's effort but the Wednesday fans didn't care, the Owls were ahead.

During a lively first-half display, Sheffield Wednesday were at least showing some passion in this fixture following their embarrassing defeat to Blackburn last Saturday. Their performance was well worthy of a lead at the break.

Rangers came at Wednesday in the remaining forty-five but Jordan Hugill and Eberechi Eze were both guilty of squandering decent opportunities.

As Sheffield Wednesday soaked up the pressure, Adam Reach found space on the left and played a perfectly timed ball into the path of Sam Winnall. He made no mistake from fourteen-yards and placed the ball neatly into the goal. Two-nil!

With victory in sight, Nahki Wells made it a nervy ending when he picked up a loose ball from Cameron Dawson; he then rounded the Wednesday keeper to score. Even so, it was little too late and the Owls were through to the next round.

This was just the response they needed after their humiliating defeat in the league. That's the magic of the cup.

Sheffield Wednesday would now face the current Premier League and FA Cup winners Manchester City in the fifth round at Hillsborough.

**Queens Park Rangers starting eleven:** Lumley, Kane, Materson, Leistner, Manning, Ball, Chair (Wells 73'), Pugh, Eze, Clarke (Osayi-Samuel 66'), Hugill.

**Sheffield Wednesday starting eleven:** Dawson, Odubajo, Lees, Börner, Fox, Murphy (Reach 72'), Hutchinson (Hunt 54'), Pelupessy, Harris, Winnall, Rhodes (Nuhiu 76').

**7.45pm Tuesday 28th January, DW Stadium (Attendance: 9,759)**

**Wigan Athletic 2-1 Sheffield Wednesday** (Murphy 32', Moore 56', Lowe 90')

Jamal Lowe snatched a late win for Wigan to sentence Sheffield Wednesday to another league defeat.

Jacob Murphy missed a glorious opportunity on the half-hour mark when he skipped past a defender but his shot was wayward. Still, the Owls winger quickly redeemed himself when he headed Wednesday in front following an inch-perfect cross from Morgan Fox on the left.

Wigan squared things up just after the interval when Kieffer Moore benefited from an error in the Owls defence, he then fired beyond Cameron Dawson.

Wednesday rode their luck on a couple of occasions

in the remaining minutes but Jacobs and Moore both missed decent chances for the hosts.

When a draw looked almost certain, Jamal Lowe ghosted into the box and looped his header over the onrushing Wednesday keeper in the ninetieth-minute. Wigan held on to take all three points.

Once again it was another underwhelming performance by the Owls in the league; this defeat was Sheffield Wednesday's fifth in their last six Championship fixtures.

Garry Monk didn't hold back after the final whistle as he began to question some of the player's work ethic in a post-match interview.

**League position:** 11th

**Wigan Athletic starting eleven:** Marshall, Byrne, Kipre, Naismith, Robinson, Morsy, Dowell (Williams 66'), Lowe, Evans (Garner 89'), Gelhardt (Jacobs 66'), Moore.

**Sheffield Wednesday starting eleven:** Dawson, Odubajo, Iorfa, Börner, Fox (Lees 51'), Murphy, Pelupessy, Bannan, Harris (Reach 71'), Winnall (Rhodes 58'), Nuhiu.

# The January Transfer Window

Prior to the January transfer window commencing and having not heard otherwise, it was presumed that Sheffield Wednesday were not under any transfer embargo whatsoever. This news came rather unexpectedly due to the on-going disagreement between the club and the English Football League over possible misconduct charges.

As a result, it was believed that the Owls were all set to trade. In such a scenario, Wednesday would most likely keep a low profile by exploring the free and loan markets as they did previously.

On New Year's Day, 1st January 2020, Sheffield Wednesday's transfer activity was under-way within hours of the window opening. Owls fans awoke to the news that Jordan Thorniley had secured a permanent move to League One outfit Blackpool for an undisclosed fee.

This trade came as a surprise to many Wednesdayites since the twenty-three-year old defender had been a regular in the Owls' development squad and featured heavily for the first-team during the 2018/19 campaign. However, Thorniley had fallen further down the pecking order under Garry Monk having only made two League Cup appearances this term.

Almost two-weeks later on the 13th January, Sheffield Wednesday sold another defender. Ash Baker completed his move to League Two side Newport County for a hidden fee. In many ways the twenty-three-year-old departed the club under similar circumstances to Thorniley. Baker had made thirteen first-team appearances for the Owls in past seasons but was yet to be selected this campaign. This transaction made perfect sense for all parties involved.

Midway through the window on the 15th January, Sheffield Wednesday captured the signature of Manuel Hidalgo from Italian side Triestina for an undisclosed fee. The Argentinian winger was the first signing under Garry Monk's reign. Having completed a successful trial period with the Owls, the twenty-year-old would most likely feature for the development squad, at least for the time being. With the short and long-term future in mind, Hidalgo was expected to keep the likes of Kadeem Harris and Adam Reach on their toes.

Like any other transfer window, many players throughout the month were rumoured to be linked with Sheffield Wednesday, yet nothing was concrete.

The clock was ticking…

Before the Owls managed to capture any other signing, Cameron Dawson signed a four-year contract extension on the 27th January. The Wednesday shot-stopper had played in twenty league and cup fixtures this season and was now a trusted member of the Owls' first-team. Tying down Dawson was met with great positivity, he was still only twenty-four-years of age and he had the ability to fight for the number one spot for years many to come.

Two-days later on the 29th January, Sheffield Wednesday signed Alessio Da Cruz on loan until the end of the season from Italian outfit Parma. The twenty-three-year-old could play out wide or in the number ten role if necessary. Da Cruz had spent the first half of the season on loan at Serie B side Ascoli where he was the scorer or creator of thirteen goals in eighteen appearances. Nonetheless, it was soon highlighted that he had been sent off on three occasions already this term. This made the arrival of Alessio all the more interesting, whether that was for good or bad reasoning, nobody knew as yet.

Even though the Owls had completed the loan signing of Da Cruz, there was still the expectation to capture at least one more signing before the window closed. Sheffield Wednesday only had forty-eight-hours left to do so.

On Thursday the 30th January, the day prior to the deadline, the Owls confirmed the signing of full-back Ryan Galvin. The eighteen-year-old had been on trial and was now a permanent member of the development squad. Despite capturing Galvin's signature, Wednesdayites remained intrigued as to what business the Owls could conclude the following day, if any.

Deadline day, Friday the 31st January had arrived. All-day the Owls faithful remained poised at the possible addition of at least one more player before the 11pm cut-off.

After what seemed like an age in waiting, Sheffield Wednesday finally confirmed the double signing of Connor Wickham and Josh Windass. Both players arrived on loan until the end of the season.

Incoming from Crystal Palace, Wickham was on his third loan stint at Sheffield Wednesday. He had previously scored nine goals in seventeen appearances between 2013 and 2014. The Owls' fans were generally overjoyed at Wickham's return. There was no doubting his ability at this level and all he needed to do now was find his feet and make an impression.

Josh Windass arrived in a similar situation to Wickham; twenty-six-years-old, attacking minded and an eye for goal. The Hull born forward was attained from Wigan Athletic and is the son of former Sheffield Wednesday pro Dean Windass.

Even though it was a little disappointing that no further players departed the club, the two deadline day swoops of Wickham and Windass ensured that the Owls' January business had been a success. It was now time for each player to let their football do the talking, given the opportunity. Sheffield Wednesday had more numbers in attack than ever and competition for a starting place was at its peak.

In what was Garry Monk's first transfer window at the helm, it was important to note that every player signed by the Owls chief was relatively young in age with a lot to prove. Likewise to Sheffield Wednesday's summer trading, their recruitment approach had been smart with little expenditure. Even so, in what is a results business the Owls now faced a tough encounter against Millwall at Hillsborough.

# The 2019/20 Campaign Continued…

### 3pm Saturday 1st February, Hillsborough (Attendance: 23,052)

### Sheffield Wednesday 0-0 Millwall

Sheffield Wednesday and Millwall had to make do with a point in this uneventful affair at Hillsborough.

The contest was monotonous as both sides lacked quality in the final third. Yet just before half-time, Wednesday came closest when a glancing header from Adam Reach went agonisingly wide.

After the introduction of Forestieri and Da Cruz in the second-half, Wednesday began to press but it was still a relatively dull showing overall. Bodvarsson had the chance to win it for the Lions but his lob was misjudged and the ball went over.

The points were shared, this scoreless draw confirmed that the Owls were now the joint lowest scorers on home soil in the Championship with fourteen goals. Furthermore, Sheffield Wednesday had still not won at Hillsborough since they beat Bristol City one-nil on the 22nd December.

Wednesday had certainly started the new decade on the back-foot, they were now sat twenty-third in the form table having only gained four points from a possible eighteen. A quick turnaround was necessary.

**League position:** 11th

**Sheffield Wednesday starting eleven:** Dawson, Odubajo, Iorfa, Börner, Palmer, Murphy (Da Cruz 67'), Pelupessy, Bannan, Harris (Forestieri 56'), Reach, Nuhiu.

**Millwall starting eleven:** Bialkowski, Romeo, Hutchinson, Cooper, Wallace, Wallace, Williams, Woods, Ferguson (Mahoney 61'), Smith (Bodvarsson 61'), Bradshaw (Molumby 79').

**1.30pm Saturday 8$^{th}$ February, Oakwell (Attendance: 17,789)**

**Barnsley 1-1 Sheffield Wednesday** (Windass 16', Woodrow 24')

Sheffield Wednesday threw away the lead to share the spoils in this South Yorkshire derby.

Both Connor Wickham and Josh Windass were named in the starting eleven and were all set to make their Sheffield Wednesday debuts.

With just over a quarter of the game gone it was one of the Owls loanees who hit the net on his first attempt. As the ball ran free in the area, Windass took a touch and unleashed a shot beyond the Barnsley keeper.

Though, Sheffield Wednesday's lead didn't last longer than eight-minutes. Cauley Woodrow made the most of a terrible clearance from Cameron Dawson as he delicately placed the ball into an empty net from thirty-five-yards.

Despite numerous chances in the second-half, neither side were clinical enough in front of goal. Alessio Da Cruz fired wide on the volley with sixty-three on the clock and Connor Wickham headed over just before he was replaced by Atdhe Nuhiu. Wednesday also rode their luck at times as the fixture edged closer to full-time.

It was honours even at Oakwell.

Unusually, the last four contests between Barnsley and Sheffield Wednesday at Oakwell had ended in one-one draws as well as both sides having a different manager on each of those occasions. Also, the Owls had now thrown away twenty points in total from winning positions this season.

Next up was a midweek trip to Luton Town who were sat at the foot of the table...

**League position:** 11th

**Barnsley starting eleven:** Collins, Williams, Soll-bauer, Anderson, Oduor, Thomas (Styles 62'), Mowatt, Simoes-Inacio (Schmidt 83'), Woodrow, Chaplin (Bahre

68'), Brown.

**Sheffield Wednesday starting eleven:** Dawson, Iorfa, Lees, Börner, Palmer, Pelupessy (Lee 66'), Bannan, Forestieri (Murphy 71'), Windass, Da Cruz, Wickham (Nuhiu 80').

## 7.45pm Wednesday 12th February, Kenilworth Road (Attendance: 10,001)

### Luton Town 1-0 Sheffield Wednesday (Collins 23')

Sheffield Wednesday slumped to another league defeat as the pressure began to mount up on Garry Monk.

The game couldn't have got off to a worse start when Luton were awarded a spot-kick with only fifteen-seconds on the clock. Fortunately for the Owls, James Collins stepped up and smashed the penalty against the crossbar. It was a huge let off.

The Hatters remained on the front foot and got their noses in front with a quarter of the game gone. Harry Cornick dispossessed Iorfa, rounded Cameron Dawson and then squared the ball to Collins. The Luton number nineteen made up for his penalty miss and side-footed the ball into the empty net.

Like most of Sheffield Wednesday's recent fixtures, it would be an uphill battle for the remainder of the tie.

The Owls best chance to level came in the second-half.

Kadeem Harris crossed the ball into the path of Julian Börner but his header went painfully wide. The Championships highest scorers on the road couldn't find a breakthrough and they were beginning to look desperate.

When the final whistle blew the Owls had lost to the division's lowest ranked side prior to kick-off. Not only that, Luton Town had lost more league games than any other side in the top four tiers. It was a torrid 2020 so far for Wednesday with only one league win in six.

**League position:** 12th

**Luton Town starting eleven:** Sluga, Bree, Pearson, Bradley, Potts, Rea, Tunnicliffe, Mpanzu, Brown (Shinnie 90+4'), Collins, Cornick (Hylton 68').

**Sheffield Wednesday starting eleven:** Dawson, Iorfa, Lees, Börner, Palmer (Murphy 71'), Lee, Bannan, Forestieri (Harris 45'), Windass (Nuhiu 61'), Da Cruz, Wickham.

### 3pm Saturday 15<sup>th</sup> February, Hillsborough (Attendance: 22,199)

**Sheffield Wednesday 0-3 Reading** (Meite 21', Urhoghide Sent Off 49', Puscas 72', Baldock Penalty 90+1')

Sheffield Wednesday were still to score at home this calender year after suffering a heavy home defeat to the Royals.

Reading hadn't won a league fixture in their previous seven but it was the away side that broke the deadlock. Ovie Ejaria played a defence splitting ball into the path of Yokou Meite, the Royals forward then slotted the ball beyond Cameron Dawson from eight-yards.

Sheffield Wednesday lacked confidence in the final third and only managed to have one shot on target in the whole first-half. Reading found themselves a goal to the good at the midway interval.

With only a handful of minutes on the clock in the second period, Osaze Urhoghide got his marching orders for a second bookable offence when he brought down Ejaria on the flank. There were no complaints and off he went.

Jacob Murphy was the only player to show a glimmer of quality when he was introduced but it wasn't enough to spark a Wednesday comeback.

To aggravate matters, Reading doubled their lead when Andy Yiadom's shot took a slight deflection off George

Puscas and the ball flew into the goal.

The Royals extended their lead again, it was in added-time when Sam Baldock converted a penalty despite Cameron Dawson making his best attempt to save. It was another bad day at the office for the Owls.

At full-time, Sheffield Wednesday had failed to score in four consecutive fixtures at Hillsborough for the first time since 2015. In fact, it was three-hundred and forty-two-minutes since their last goal on home soil. Additionally, Urhoghide's sending off was the Owls' fifth red in total of the league campaign which was more than any other Championship side at the time.

The Owls were now sat firmly at the bottom of the form table having only collected five points from a possible thirty.

**League position:** 12th

**Sheffield Wednesday starting eleven:** Dawson, Urhoghide, Iorfa, Börner, Palmer, Pelupessy (Bannan 45'), Lee, Da Cruz (Murphy 56'), Forestieri, Harris, Nuhiu (Wickham 68').

**Reading starting eleven:** Cabral Barbosa, Yiadom, Morrison, Moore, Richards, Rinomhota, Swift, Meite, Olise (Adam 68'), Ejaria (Masika 86'), Puscas (Baldock 83').

**3pm Saturday 22<sup>nd</sup> February, St. Andrews (Attendance: 22,120)**

**Birmingham City 3-3 Sheffield Wednesday** (Murphy Own Goal 6', Bannan 20', Jutkiewicz 30', Forestieri Penalty 34', Murphy 65', Hogan 90+1')

A late Birmingham City goal denied Garry Monk a winning return to his old club in this six goal thriller.

Birmingham scored early on in the tie when the ball was whipped into the mixer from a corner. At his despair, Jacob Murphy's attempt to clear the ball was directed into his own goal.

Despite the element of misfortune that was just the start Wednesday could've done without given their recent results in the league.

Wednesday trailed until the twentieth-minute before Barry Bannan took aim from distance and drilled the ball past Lee Camp. It was a great response after their earlier setback.

Ten-minutes later, City regained the lead. After some positive forward play, Lukas Jutkiewicz found space on the edge of the area and fired beyond Cameron Dawson from twenty-yards. The contest had been full of energy so far and this goal wasn't the last during the opening forty-five.

Kadeem Harris skipped by a couple of defenders on the left and succeeding his cross, Kieran Lee was consequently tripped. The referee quickly pointed to the spot. Fernando Forestieri was the designated kick-taker and he managed to hold his nerve, the South American comfortably guided the ball to the left of Lee Camp and into the goal. Two-two!

Sheffield Wednesday then took the lead for the first time in this entertaining tie. Forestieri found Jacob Murphy in space on the right before the Owls loanee smashed his shot beyond Camp. It was a brilliant finish.

Wednesday were full of confidence, Murphy and Wickham both had opportunities to seal the win for the Owls but Camp was equal to their efforts.

Moments after the fourth-official had indicated there would be four-minutes of added-time, Birmingham City found an equaliser. Scott Hogan finished emphatically following a superb knock-down. Typical!

The match ended in a draw. Sheffield Wednesday had still not beaten the Blues in six attempts since their last victory in February 2017.

Strangely enough, Wednesday had now scored more goals on the road again than any other side in the Championship with thirty in total. On the flip side, they had still scored the least amount of goals on home soil in the division with fourteen. That's just the Wednesday way.

**League position:** 12th

**Birmingham City starting eleven:** Camp, Colin, Roberts, Clarke-Salter (Dean 77'), Pedersen, Bela (Montero 82'), Gardner, Sunjic (Crowley 69'), Belliingham, Hogan, Jutkiewicz.

**Sheffield Wednesday starting eleven:** Dawson, Pelupessy (Wickham 45'), Lees, Iorfa (Fox 45'), Börner, Palmer, Murphy, Lee, Bannan, Harris, Forestieri (Fletcher 72').

### 7.45pm Wednesday 26th February, Hillsborough (Attendance: 21,370)

### Sheffield Wednesday 1-0 Charlton Athletic (Fletcher 90+5')

A Steven Fletcher goal in stoppage-time was enough to end Sheffield Wednesday's seven match winless run.

The Owls looked the more likely scorers in the first-half, mainly due to the fact that Forestieri was looking lively in the forward line. The striker created a couple of chances for himself in the opening half-hour but both of his efforts were equally matched by Phillips in the Charlton sticks.

Despite the Owls bossing the play, the tie was goalless at the break. To Wednesday's credit also, the away side had failed to have a shot on target during the first period.

When the fixture restarted, Sheffield Wednesday created three chances in quick succession but Forestieri, Wickham and Harris all failed to find the net.

As Charlton continued to ride their luck, Fletcher had a couple of golden opportunities to score but Phillips pulled off two fantastic saves.

Minutes later, Lyle Taylor rattled the Owls crossbar from distance with a thunderous effort. That was a quick reminder that this contest could've still gone either way.

Having already had twenty-three efforts at goal during the ninety, Wednesday floated the ball into the box in what was a last-ditch attempt to score. Fletcher made a nuisance of himself and reacted quickly to head home from close range. The Owls players, management staff and fans were overcome with joy. There was no way back for Charlton, Wednesday had snatched all the points.

Prior to this goal, Sheffield Wednesday were the last side to score at home in 2020 across all four of English football's top tiers. Thankfully, they had now scored and won at Hillsborough for the first time since the turn of the new decade. What a relief!

**League position:** 12th

**Sheffield Wednesday starting eleven:** Dawson, Palmer, Lees, Börner, Fox, Murphy, Lee, Bannan, Harris (Fletcher 57'), Wickham (Nuhiu 75'), Forestieri (Da Cruz 79').

**Charlton Athletic starting eleven:** Phillips, Matthews,

Lockyer, Pearce, Doughty, Oshilaja, Cullen, Davis, Oztumer (Lapslie 56'), Bone (Green 75'), Taylor.

**3pm Saturday 29<sup>th</sup> February, Hillsborough (Attendance: 25,148)**

**Sheffield Wednesday 1-3 Derby County** (Lawrence 7', Lawrence 24', Knight 30', Windass 74')

The Owls handed the victory to the travelling Rams in what was a torrid first-half display.

The visitors scored early on in the tie when Tom Lawrence's shot took an unfortunate deflection to wrong foot Cameron Dawson before hitting the net.

With just over a quarter of the game gone, Lawrence scored again for County. With Wednesday sloppy in possession, the Derby forward capitalised by taking aim and finishing into the bottom corner.

Wednesday were masters of their own downfall as Jason Knight added a third when he fired in off the post from a tight angle. In what was a shambolic display so far by the Owls, some of the Wednesday faithful had already left the stadium as the tie edged closer to half-time.

The Owls did improve during the second-half and had to wait until the seventy-fourth-minute to get on the score-sheet. Jacob Murphy whipped a cross into the box before Josh Windass got his foot to the ball and scored from close range.

At full-time, Derby County had only lost two of their past twenty-two league fixtures against the Owls and had now won back-to-back games at Hillsborough for the first time since 2009. Sheffield Wednesday's record against the Rams was appalling but it was fair to say that they had no complaints on this occasion, they had been soundly beaten.

**League position:** 12th

**Sheffield Wednesday starting eleven:** Dawson, Palmer, Lees (Iorfa 45'), Börner, Fox, Murphy, Lee, Bannan, Harris (Wickham 39'), Forestieri, Fletcher (Windass 45').

**Derby County starting eleven:** Hamer, Wisdom, Bogle, Clarke, Forsyth, Knight (Davies 58'), Bird, Rooney, Lawrence, Waghorn (Marriott 77'), Martin (Shinnie 76').

**FA Cup Round Five - 7.45pm Wednesday 4th March, Hillsborough (Attendance: 20,995)**

**Sheffield Wednesday 0-1 Manchester City** (Aguero 53')

Sergio Aguero scored the only goal of the game to end Sheffield Wednesday's valiant FA Cup run.

Although the Owls sat deep they made a promising start during the early stages. Jacob Murphy cut inside on his left-foot and shot narrowly wide with seven-minutes on the clock.

From then on City had most of the possession for the remainder of the game. They came closest in the opening period when Otamendi headed against the crossbar.

The current Premier League and FA Cup holders continued to probe but couldn't find a breakthrough before the interval.

Five-minutes after the restart the away side hit the woodwork for the second time in the tie, the ball was played out wide to Mendy who unleashed his shot from the edge of the area and rattled the bar.

Soon after City's persistence paid off. Following a ball into the box, Aguero swivelled and powered his effort towards goal. Wildsmith's attempt to save needed a stronger hand as the ball looped over the Wednesday shot-stopper and into the net.

It was one-way traffic throughout, the Owls keeper faced twenty shots during the ninety and had to pull off numerous saves to keep Wednesday in the contest.

With little time remaining, Steven Fletcher couldn't quite stretch far enough to finish off a cross from Alex Hunt. The referee blew the final whistle shortly after.

Wednesday had been outplayed but it had been a resolute effort against one of the world's best.

**Sheffield Wednesday starting eleven:** Wildsmith, Palmer, Iorfa, Börner (Lees 45'), Fox, Pelupessy, Murphy, Lee (Hunt 63'), Bannan, Da Cruz, Forestieri (Fletcher

56').

**Manchester City starting eleven:** Bravo, Cancelo, Stones, Otamendi, Mendy, Bernardo Silva, Rodri, Silva, Mahrez, Aguero (Sterling 86'), Gabriel Jesus.

**3pm Saturday 7<sup>th</sup> March, Griffin Park (Attendance: 12,273)**

**Brentford 5-0 Sheffield Wednesday** (Dasilva 10', Marcondes 18', Mbeumo 40', Dasilva 73', Fosu-Henry 82')

Promotion pushing Brentford thumped five past a sorry Sheffield Wednesday.

The home side were unforgiving from the off. Ollie Watkins hit the bar from a first time shot with seven-minutes gone. Josh Dasilva then gave Brentford the lead when the Bees' number fourteen volleyed home following lack-lustre parry from Cameron Dawson.

The Owls found themselves two goals down inside of twenty-minutes, Emiliano Marcondes took aim on the edge of the area and curled the ball with precision into the top corner of Wednesday's goal. It was a fantastic finish and a two goal advantage was nothing more than Brentford deserved.

Wednesday began to penetrate in stages before the interval but efforts from Da Cruz, Fletcher and Windass all went begging.

Bryan Mbeumo scored Brentford's third with five-minutes remaining in the first-half. A delightful ball was played through to the Bees forward before he guided his shot past Dawson. It was far too comfortable for the hosts.

The second-half was uneventful until Brentford stepped it up another gear. Dasilva managed to turn in the box and finished with ease when through on goal, that was the Bees' fourth of the afternoon and it only got worse for Wednesday.

Fosu-Henry made it five when he drilled his shot through the legs of Dominic Iorfa and into the bottom right corner of the net. It was men versus boys, Brentford were a class above their counterparts.

When the final whistle blew, the Owls had slipped to the bottom half of the league table for the first time this season and this was Wednesday's second five-nil defeat of the campaign.

The fans were losing their patience, primarily because the Owls were sat just nine points above the relegation zone.

**League position:** 15th

**Brentford starting eleven:** Raya, Dalsgaard, Jeanvier, Pinnock, Henry, Marcondes, Norgaard (Baptiste 78'), Dasilva (Valencia Castillo 84'), Mbeumo (Fosu-Henry 79'), Watkins, Benrahma.

**Sheffield Wednesday starting eleven:** Dawson, Palmer, Iorfa, Lees, Fox, Pelupessy, Murphy, Windass (Wickham 45'), Bannan, Da Cruz (Forestieri 45'), Fletcher (Harris 65').

# THE CORONAVIRUS PANDEMIC

*Extraordinary And Unprecedented*

S ucceeding the start of a global coronavirus pandemic, the English Football League suspended all
fixtures between 14th March until the 3rd April
at the earliest. This sensible decision was announced
as a precautionary measure due to the fact that the un-
treatable virus was continuing to spread throughout
the country and it's footballing network.

With British football now on shut-down and with
the health and well-being at the forefront of people's
minds, medical experts advised the worldwide popu-
lation who had contracted the virus to self-isolate for
a two-week period. As a result, many football clubs

promptly acted upon this advice as players and staff remained at home until a full recovery was made.

This unprecedented situation meant that lots of question remained unanswered except for the fact that football will always be second to public health, and rightly so. Safety was of paramount importance.

Sheffield Wednesday's fixtures with Nottingham Forest, Bristol City and West Bromwich Albion were now delayed until further notice.

As the situation worsened over time and with new government measures for the public becoming controlled, all major sporting events across the globe were either cancelled or postponed. The most notable was the 2020 Tokyo Olympic games and the 2020 European Championships, both competitions were due to commence over the summer but were now delayed for twelve-months.

The most crucial of news in the footballing calender came on the 19th March. The English Football League extended the suspension of all fixtures until the 30th April at the earliest and confirmed that the 2019/20 season would be extended indefinitely if necessary. In other words, the end of this league campaign would conclude but at this stage nobody was any the wiser as to when this may be. All remaining fixtures were now postponed.

This new criteria soon became a worry for the lower and semi-professional sides who were struggling to pay staff and player wages due to the dramatic halt on gate receipts. In this period of uncertainty, it was just a waiting game to see if football clubs across the nation could survive this year financially after a dramatic squeeze on the economy.

When the 1st April arrived, Sheffield Wednesday were one of many clubs who placed a significant number of employees on furlough leave as part of the governments new job retention scheme. With the stadium and training facilities on lock-down, numerous staff members were unable to carry out their normal duties if they couldn't work from home.

It was at this point that Dejphon Chansiri pledged to top-up the pay of all furloughed workers to one-hundred-percent of their salary rather than the regular eighty-percent that was to be reimbursed by the government. This act was a fantastic gesture by the Owls Chairman and it was met with overwhelming encouragement by the fans.

As time passed, increasing pressure mounted on the English Football League to come to some arrangement over how the 2019/20 campaign would be concluded. It was even suggested that fixtures may have to be played behind closed doors if the season was to resume.

With the month of May fast approaching, speculation in the media then began to suggest that no more fixtures would commence at all. In such a scenario, opinions on how to conclude the current campaign were quickly gathering.

To decide the final league standings by a points per game average was probably the most popular choice, however this pick didn't consider the financial aspects of the game such as TV rights and season ticket refunds. It also seemed unfair to either promote or relegate a team without the completion of a full competitive league campaign. This was one hell of a conundrum for the English Football League to resolve.

A few weeks later and subject to government protocols, it was confirmed that all Premier League and Championship clubs could return to training on the 25th May. Such guidelines required each club to appoint a coronavirus officer for testing purposes and all players and staff had to adhere to 'social distancing' rules around the training ground. If successful, 'full contact' training was planned to commence a week or so later.

All of these fresh measures were put in place ahead of the newly proposed 2019/20 season restart which was set for the 12th June. If this proposal was to go ahead, there was now some light at the end of the tunnel in terms of 'normality' on the competitive football stage. Nevertheless, mass numbers of people still remained sceptical of this proposition due to a possible second wave of the virus.

Consequently, it was on the 21st May when the English Football League updated their recommended framework to determine if the 2019/20 term would resume at all. With League Two already curtailed, all Championship clubs now had the opportunity to vote for curtailment too, or alternatively for the competitive restart as proposed. Fans of all teams throughout the country eagerly awaited the result.

Meanwhile, as clubs returned to 'social distancing' training on the $25^{th}$ May, the first round of coronavirus testing took place within the same week. Only two of one-thousand and fourteen players and staff from Championship sides had tested positive. It was later confirmed that neither of these individuals represented Sheffield Wednesday.

As more rounds of testing continued within the space of a week, there was a spike in contractions. Round two saw three players or staff from two clubs test positive and round three saw ten players or staff test positive across eight clubs.

With the evidence so far suggesting that the virus was still uncontrollable, it came as quite a shock on the $31^{st}$ May when the English Football League announced that football would return behind closed doors. Still, the new date was now set for the $20^{th}$ June rather than the initially proposed date of $12^{th}$ June, and this was all in the assumption that the season wasn't to be curtailed.

With the mandatory rounds of coronavirus testing under-way at each club on a regular basis, it was on the $3^{rd}$ June when Sheffield Wednesday declared their first official positive case. The Owls member of staff who was unnamed would have to follow the government guidelines on self-isolation before returning to work when it was safe to do so. It was at this stage that well wishes rang around the club in support of the member of staff with the infection.

As the coronavirus pandemic continued to take centre-stage in the news due to it's ongoing detrimental effect on people's livelihood, there was still a heap of confusion surrounding the changing regulations that had been set by the footballing authorities because of this unprecedented situation. Players who were out of contract or loans expired at the end of this season became a hot topic at the beginning of June due to the fact that the competitive league campaign had still not been finalised. It was now a question whether or not these players would be released at the end of the month, or otherwise sign a brief contract renewal to either extend their loan spell or stay with the club until at least the present season was over.

To put this into some context in terms of numbers, the Owls had a minimum of twenty-one players on their books that were eligible to leave at the end of June or at the beginning of July. Some of those players included Paul Jones, Morgan Fox, Osaze Urhoghide, Matt Penney, Connor Kirby, Kieran Lee, Sam Hutchinson, Joey Pelupessy, Steven Fletcher, Atdhe Nuhiu, Sam Winnall, Fernando Forestieri, Jack Lee, Connor Kirby, Fraser Preston and Jack Stobbs. Not to forget those who were also on loan, David Bates, Jacob Murphy, Alessio Da Cruz, Josh Windass and Connor Wickham.

Without further ado on the 4$^{th}$ June, a trio of twelve-month contract extensions was announced, the first was Joey Pelupessy. Despite the central-midfielder originally being a bit-part-player he had slowly worked his way into the first-team under Garry Monk, so far he had made seventeen appearances in all competitions.

Osaze Urhoghide had also committed his stay with the Owls, the nineteen-year-old was one of Sheffield Wednesday's shining lights since the turn of the new year and had made four appearances in the starting-eleven.

Finally, Matt Penney signed on the dotted line even though he was still on loan until the end of the current campaign with St. Pauli and hadn't featured for the Owls since November 2018.

All three of these contract renewals were seen as commendable if you were to bare in mind that Sheffield Wednesday still didn't know what division they would be playing in next season. It was seven-months since the start of the ongoing battle between Sheffield Wednesday and the English Football League over the potential misconduct charges. The threat of a possible points deduction was still a major concern. The Owls' fate now lay in the hands of an independent disciplinary commission, but the whole scenario and its outcome was still a guessing game.

Then, the all important news that everyone had been waiting for broke on the 9th June. League One clubs had voted for curtailment and joined League Two in announcing its promoted and relegated sides by using the unweighted points per game average to determine the final league standings. Additionally, the play-offs had been given the go ahead to ascertain who would be the only other promoted side in each of those divisions.

Regardless of the dramatic conclusion in League One and Two, it was a completely different set of circumstances in the Championship. The English Football League had given the green light to a full competitive restart. Subsequently, a new schedule of fixtures was released and Sheffield Wednesday were set to lock horns with Nottingham Forest at Hillsborough just eleven-days later.

With the Championship now on track to resume, there were a set of off-field rule changes to accommodate with the condition and fitness of each team. In what was going to be a heavy programme of fixtures over a five-week period, match-day squads were to increase from eighteen to twenty and the typical maximum substitutions of three players during a tie was increased to five for each side. Drinks breaks became compulsory and hand-shakes were prohibited at all times before, during and after the tie.

Additionally, as all upcoming fixtures were set to be played behind closed doors, it was at this point that most clubs offered season-ticket holders with either pro-rata rebate options or an online streaming pass for the remaining home and away league ties. Not only that, many matches in the Premier League and Championship were made readily available to watch across numerous subscription and non-subscription platforms. The season restart certainly looked like it was going to more than make up for the cancellation of the 2020 European Championships, it seemed.

It was not until later in the month of June when we learnt the status of each player whose contract was due to expire. Paul Jones, Kieran Lee and Atdhe Nuhiu would all remain at the club until the end of the current league term having signed short term extensions. Loanees Jacob Murphy, Alessio Da Cruz, Josh Windass and Connor Wickham would also stay on at Hillsborough for the remaining nine games after the Owls had come to an agreement with their parent clubs. However David Bates, who had only made one appearance all season, returned to Hamburg.

The most startling news of all was that two of Sheffield Wednesday's most consistent performers this season, Steven Fletcher and Morgan Fox, were set to leave. Both players had racked up four player of the month awards between them this term and with Fletcher notching thirteen goals too, many Wednesday fans were under the assumption that they would remain at S6 for at least another season. Consequently and without dwelling on the matter, both players were released. Fernando Forestieri, Sam Winnall, Sam Hutchinson, Connor Kirby, Fraser Preston and Jack Stobbs were the other handful of noteworthy individuals who became free agents also.

As Garry Monk turned his attention to matters on the field, the 2019/20 season restart was just days away.

Sheffield Wednesday were hoping to quickly put to bed the fact that they had the second worst league form in the Championship since the turn of the new year. The Owls had only won two league games in 2020 so far and even though their last league encounter was over three-months ago, it was that spiritless five-nil drubbing at Brentford.

Sat fifteenth in the table, Wednesday were just nine points above the relegation zone but only eight points adrift of the play-offs with nine games remaining. If the Owls were to avoid a points deduction between now and the end of the season, their destiny was in their own hands.

Anything could happen...

# The 2019/20 Campaign Continued…

### 3pm Saturday 20ᵗʰ June, Hillsborough (Behind closed doors)

**Sheffield Wednesday 1-1 Nottingham Forest** (Lolley 69'), (Wickham 90+3')

Nottingham Forest were denied all three points as Connor Wickham found an equaliser for the Owls in added-time.

One-hundred and five-days after their last league encounter and without a soul in attendance, Sheffield Wednesday stepped onto the Hillsborough turf to get the game under-way.

The Owls showed plenty of desire to get forward in the opening forty-five-minutes but Luongo, Lee, Rhodes and Wickham were all guilty of missing half-chances in and around the area. The contest was level at the break.

It was Forest who looked encouraging when the match restarted but it was Wednesday who should've taken the lead just before the hour. Connor Wickham hit the post with a header before Kieran Lee's shot was spectacularly stopped by Joe Worrall on the goal-line.

Soon after, Wednesday were caught out when a long ball fell to Joe Lolley. The winger brought the ball down, made his way into the box and superbly placed his effort into the bottom corner of Wildsmith's goal.

Garry Monk made use of his five substitutions in second period but the Owls were still incapable of hitting the net. Kadeem Harris did go down in the box as Wednesday tried to salvage a point but the referee was having none of it.

With little or no time remaining, Alessio Da Cruz swung a delightful ball into the box from a corner only for Connor Wickham to plant his header into the angle of the Forest goal. That was Wickham's first for Sheffield Wednesday during his current loan spell.

The Owls had left it late but both sides were deserving of a point overall. Sheffield Wednesday had still only lost one of their last eleven encounters versus Nottingham Forest.

**League position: 15th**

**Sheffield Wednesday starting eleven:** Wildsmith, Palmer, Iorfa, Börner, Lee (Reach 74'), Murphy (Odubajo 68'), Rhodes (Fletcher 68') (Da Cruz 74'), Bannan, Harris, Luongo (Hunt 83'), Wickham.

**Nottingham Forest starting eleven:** Samba, Cash, Figueiredo, Worrall, Ribeiro, Johnson (Semedo 62'), Yates, Lolley, Silva (Bostock 85'), Ameobi (da Costa Joia 62'), Grabban (Diakhaby 90+1').

**12pm Sunday 28<sup>th</sup> June, Ashton Gate (Behind closed doors)**

**Bristol City 1-2 Sheffield Wednesday** (Wickham 13', Luongo 59', Wells 69')

Sheffield Wednesday put a serious dent in Bristol City's play-off hopes as the Owls moved to within three points of their challengers.

With only five-minutes on the clock, Joe Wildsmith pulled off a remarkable one-handed point-blank reflex save when Nathan Baker headed towards the Wednesday net.

Before long, Wildsmith was rewarded for his save when Connor Wickham found space in the area pending a Jacob Murphy delivery. The front-man connected with the ball and wonderfully directed his header into the Robins' goal to score his second in as many games.

To Wednesday's credit they continued to press and scored a second on the hour. The City defence failed to clear the ball before Luongo pounced and found the net from eight-yards.

The Owls were in their comfort zone until Bristol City clawed one back. Nahki Wells finished off the rebound of a spectacular Wildsmith save with just over twenty-minutes remaining. Wednesday suddenly had a game on their hands.

Garry Monk was quick to make defensive substitutions

to help see out the game and despite the six-minutes of added-time, the Owls held on. When the whistle blew, Sheffield Wednesday had beaten Bristol City in each of their last four encounters.

This was a huge win on the road which saw Wednesday climb two places in the standings.

**League position: 13th**

**Bristol City starting eleven:** Maenpaa, Hunt (Vyner 89'), Williams, Baker, Dasilva, Weimann (Nagy 65'), Massengo (Eliasson 56'), Smith, O'Dowda (Paterson 89'), Afobe (Diedhiou 64'), Wells.

**Sheffield Wednesday starting eleven:** Wildsmith, Palmer, Iorfa, Börner (Fox 45'), Lee, Murphy (Odubajo 75'), Rhodes (Da Cruz 61'), Bannan, Harris, Luongo (Pelupessy 75'), Wickham (Nuhiu 82').

**7.45pm Wednesday 1$^{st}$ July, Hillsborough (Behind closed doors)**

**Sheffield Wednesday 0-3 West Bromwich Albion** (Austin Penalty 37', Pereira 58', Pereira 85')

Sheffield Wednesday suffered their first defeat since the restart as West Brom kept up their automatic promotion fight.

The Owls settled into the game and looked full of confidence but it was the Baggies who got their noses in front from the spot. Odubajo was ruled to have fouled O'Shea in the area and Charlie Austin did the rest from twelve-yards.

The away side found the net again just before the hour when Pereira headed home from a Kieran Gibbs cross. The Owls had it all to do if they were to get anything from this game.

Wednesday were looking for a quick response and they almost pulled a goal back when Kadeem Harris fancied his luck from outside the box, but his curling effort came crashing back off the post.

The blue and white forward line huffed and puffed but too much damage had already been inflicted. Pereira grabbed his second of the evening when his powerful left-foot shot found its way past Wildsmith. Game over.

On the balance of play a three-nil scoreline didn't reflect the game at all. Garry Monk and his men had to take this result on the chin. On to the next one.

**League position: 13th**

**Sheffield Wednesday starting eleven:** Wildsmith, Odubajo, Iorfa, Palmer, Murphy, Luongo (Lee 62'), Bannan (Hunt 87'), Harris, Reach (Nuhiu 62'), Rhodes (Da Cruz 45'), Wickham.

**West Bromwich Albion starting eleven:** Johnstone, O'Shea, Bartley, Hegazi, Gibbs, Harper (Ajayi 88'), Sawyers, Pereira (Livermore 88'), Krovinovic (Robson-

Kanu 69'), Diangana (Robinson 55'), Austin (Grosicki 69').

## 12pm Sunday 5th July, Liberty Stadium (Behind closed doors)

**Swansea City 2-1 Sheffield Wednesday** (Brewster 52', Ayew Penalty 66', Nuhiu 90+4)

The Swans punished the Owls with two goals in the second-half although Atdhe Nuhiu did make it a tense finale for the hosts.

Jacob Murphy looked threatening on the right in the early stages but he was unable to hit the net on a couple of occasions.

With both defences on top in the first-half the tie was goalless at the break.

In the second-half, Swansea broke the deadlock when Rhian Brewster smashed the ball beyond Wildsmith from a Connor Roberts delivery. Wednesday only had themselves to blame as the cross should've been dealt with.

It only got worse for the Owls when the Welsh side were awarded a penalty in the sixty-fifth minute. Adam Reach made a clumsy challenge in the area before Andre Ayew converted a left-foot shot into the bottom right corner.

Wednesday had to go for it and did manage to score a consolation goal in stoppage-time, Jacob Murphy was the provider when Nuhiu headed beyond Woodman in the Swansea sticks. That was the 'big' man's fifth of the season and all of his goals this term had still come in added-time.

A full-time, Wednesday had still not won at Swansea since August 1983 and they were now sat eight points above the drop zone with only five games remaining.

**League position:** 14th

**Swansea City starting eleven:** Woodman, Roberts, Naughton, Guehi, Bidwell, Grimes, Fulton, Routledge (van der Hoorn 63'), Gallagher (Byers 70') , Ayew, Brewster (Cullen 88').

**Sheffield Wednesday starting eleven:** Wildsmith, Palmer, Iorfa, Börner, Murphy, Bannan, Luongo (Nuhiu 70'), Reach (Harris 67'), Lee (Hunt 45'), Da Cruz (Rhodes 79'), Wickham.

## 7.45pm Wednesday 8<sup>th</sup> July, Hillsborough (Behind closed doors)

**Sheffield Wednesday 1-3 Preston North-End** (Murphy 58', Sinclair 78', Stockley 87', Potts 90+6')

Preston scored three late goals to secure their first win in seven which saw the Owls drop to their lowest league position of the season.

Wednesday were unlucky not to score the opener just minutes after kick-off when Dominic Iorfa's header rattled the crossbar following a Barry Bannan corner. From then on, Preston created chance after chance but were wasteful in front of goal.

It wasn't until the second-half when the first goal of the tie was scored. Murphy drove forward and played a tidy one-two with Nuhiu on the edge of the area before the Wednesday loanee fired his shot into the bottom left corner of the net.

The away side pulled a goal back twenty-minutes later when a flicked Jayden Stockley header fell into the path of Scott Sinclair. He twisted in the area to create a shooting opportunity before neatly placing his shot beyond Wildsmith.

Julian Börner thought he'd scored the winner for Wednesday when he headed home with only a handful of minutes remaining but the linesman soon raised his flag. Preston then went straight to other end of the park and grabbed a likely winner when Stockley's instinctive right-foot shot from outside the area flew into the goal. It was cruel couple of minutes for the Owls.

Preston showed no remorse and added a third in injury-time when Brad Potts scored with an effort from twenty-yards. All three of their goals had been scored by an Alex Neil substitute.

The Owls had now lost three games on the bounce and that was the end of Sheffield Wednesday's winning streak of five in a row against North-End.

**League position:** 16th

**Sheffield Wednesday starting eleven:** Wildsmith, Palmer, Iorfa, Börner, Murphy (Odubajo 64'), Pelupessy, Bannan, Luongo, Harris (Reach 88'), Nuhiu, Da Cruz (Windass 70').

**Preston North-End starting eleven:** Rudd, Rafferty, Bauer, Davies, Hughes (Sinclair 76'), Pearson (Johnson 65'), Ledson (Potts 65'), Maguire (Stockley 76'), Browne, Storey, Barkhuizen (Gallagher 83').

**3pm Saturday 11<sup>th</sup> July, Kiyan Prince Foundation Stadium (Behind closed doors)**

**Queens Park Rangers 0-3 Sheffield Wednesday** (Iorfa 5', Windass 45+2', Murphy 78')

On the day after Jack Charlton's passing, Sheffield Wednesday did him proud with a soothing victory at Queens Park Rangers expense.

The Owls found the net not long after kick-off when an initial Josh Windass set-piece was saved. Massimo Luongo then hit the rebound onto the post only for Dominic Iorfa to place the ball into the Rangers goal on the follow up. Advantage Wednesday.

Monk's troops bossed the first-half and grabbed a second on the stroke of half-time when Windass glanced home on the goal-line from a Da Cruz corner.

When the second-half got under-way, Windass continued to spark fear in the Rangers defence and he did everything but add to his tally. Wednesday were cruising and they could've had five or six.

Substitute Jacob Murphy scored the Owls third when Barry Bannan played a dinked through-ball to the Wednesday forward before he composed himself and beautifully fired past Joe Lumley. Yes!

That was game, set and match. Wednesday had managed to keep a clean sheet on the road for the first time since their two-nil victory at Leeds United. This win was probably the most complete performance by the Owls since the turn of the year which saw them move ten points clear of the drop zone.

**League position:** 14th

**Queens Park Rangers starting eleven:** Lumley, Materson (Oteh 33'), Cameron, Barbet, Kakay, Amos, Ball (Clarke 60'), Manning, Eze, Shodipo (Chair 60'), Osayi-Samuel.

**Sheffield Wednesday starting eleven:** Wildsmith, Iorfa, Lees (Shaw 74'), Börner, Odubajo, Hunt (Pelupessy 61'), Bannan, Luongo, Harris, Windass (Nuhiu 74'), Da Cruz (Murphy 55').

**7.45pm Tuesday 14<sup>th</sup> July, Hillsborough (Behind closed doors)**

**Sheffield Wednesday 0-0 Huddersfield Town**

Sheffield Wednesday kept their second clean sheet in a row but it was both Yorkshire sides who failed to find the net during this frustrating encounter.

It was the visitors who started the brighter but they didn't make the most of their opportunities in the opening quarter.

As the Owls grew in confidence, Moses Odubajo and Kadeem Harris created the best chances of the half but Jonas Lossl had to make strong saves on each occasion.

Wednesday continued to live dangerously in the second-half and it was hard to see the tie remaining goalless for much longer.

The Owls did apply the pressure but it was the Terriers who should've scored with ten-minutes remaining. Following a cross and with the goal at his mercy, Fraizer Campbell blazed over from six-yards.

With a lack of quality in front of goal and once the four-minutes of injury-time had passed, the points were shared.

This result ensured Sheffield Wednesday remained unbeaten against Huddersfield Town in their previous nine league meetings.

**League position:** 15th

**Sheffield Wednesday starting eleven:** Wildsmith, Iorfa, Lees, Börner, Odubajo, Hunt (Pelupessy 58'), Bannan, Luongo (Reach 70'), Harris, Windass (Nuhiu 70'), Murphy (Da Cruz 58').

**Huddersfield Town starting eleven:** Lossl, Chalobah, Stearman, Schindler, Toffolo, Hogg, O'Brien, Kachunga (Willock 70'), Smith Rowe, Grant, Mounie (Campbell 78').

**3pm Saturday 18<sup>th</sup> July, Craven Cottage (Behind closed doors)**

**Fulham 5-3 Sheffield Wednesday** (Kebano 11', Mitrovic Penalty 26', Mitrovic 41', Nuhiu Penalty 49', Kebano 73', Murphy 78', Nuhiu 89', De Cordova-Reid 90+1', Reed Sent Off 90+5')

Fulham came out on top during this action packed penultimate game of the season.

Neeskens Kebano scored for Fulham with their first shot of the game when the wide man cut inside from the left and hit a precise effort beyond Wildsmith from twenty-yards.

The Cottagers then took the game by the scruff of the neck and added a second when a Josh Onomah through ball found Mitrovic in acres of space before he took aim and hit the net.

Fulham made it three-nil when the referee pointed to the spot just before the interval. Kebano had drawn a foul from Dominic Iorfa and Mitrovic made no mistake from twelve-yards.

The Owls pulled a goal back just minutes into the second-half when Jacob Murphy was tussled to the ground as he closed in on goal. Nuhiu stepped up and scored with a cool finish to his left. That was Atdhe's first goal this term that had come in 'normal time' having scored his previous five after the ninety-minute mark.

Fulham remained in control and scored their fourth from a set-piece from just outside the area. Kebano was the designated taker and he left Wildsmith flat-footed when he cheekily rolled the ball underneath the wall and into the goal.

The goals kept on coming. Jacob Murphy tried his luck when the ball fell to him on the edge of the box, it was a soft attempt but it hit the net after a wicked deflection. That was Murphy's eighth of the season.

Nuhiu was at the double and made it a nail-biting climax for the hosts. He headed home following a Jacob Murphy cross and there was still seven-minutes of injury-time left to play. That was goal number fifty for the striker in what was the seventh year of his current Owls career.

Still, Wednesday's hope for a draw was quickly dashed as Fulham responded almost instantly when De Cordova-Reid fired past Wildsmith from outside of the area.

Moments later and just to add to the drama, Harrison Reed was dismissed after a second bookable offence.

Sheffield Wednesday's unbeaten run in their last three visits to Craven Cottage had come to an end. That defeat also confirmed the Owls had only won three of their last eighteen fixtures.

**League position:** 16th

**Fulham starting eleven:** Rodak, Christie, Hector, Le Marchand, Ream, Arter (Odoi 90'), Johansen (Reed 68'), Knockaert (Sessegnon 90'), Onomah (Cairney 79'), Kebano (De Cordova-Reid 78'), Mitrovic.

**Sheffield Wednesday starting eleven:** Wildsmith, Iorfa, Lees, Börner, Odubajo (Murphy 45'), Pelupessy (Hunt 79'), Bannan, Luongo (Reach 75'), Harris, Windass (Wickham 45'), Da Cruz (Nuhiu 45').

**7.30pm Wednesday 22nd July, Hillsborough (Behind closed doors)**

**Sheffield Wednesday 1-2 Middlesbrough** (Murphy 10', McNair 22', Assombalonga 90+3')

Sheffield Wednesday suffered a loss on the final day when Britt Assombalonga hit a stoppage-time winner.

Boro almost opened the scoring when Paddy McNair's shot from outside the area smashed against Wildsmith's post before rebounding clear of any further danger.

Shortly after, Jacob Murphy cut inside on the right and unleashed a shot from twenty-yards, the ball took a huge deflection and looped over Stojanovic in the visitors goal. Unbelievably, that was the Owls' first goal in the opening forty-five minutes at Hillsborough in 2020.

The away side then found an equaliser with a quarter of the game gone. Marcus Tavernier set-up the unmarked McNair with a left-field cross who then placed the ball with ease into the back of the net.

Middlesbrough were showing more intent since scoring but the contest was all square at the break.

Wednesday improved during the second-half and almost scored what could've been a winner with five-minutes left on the clock. Iorfa crossed low and from a promising position Jacob Murphy hit wide of the post.

It was deep into added-time when Boro nicked it. Ashley Fletcher delivered a low cross into the box before Assombalonga created enough room to fire off a shot, Wildsmith got a palm to the ball but it was too powerful and trickled into the goal.

That was that, the referee called an end to the 2019/20 season and for many players this fixture would've been their last outing in Wednesday colours.

The Owls' campaign had ended on a knife-edge due to the unknown verdict of the independent disciplinary commission...

**Final league position:** 16th (Subject to change)

**Sheffield Wednesday starting eleven:** Wildsmith, Iorfa, Lees, Palmer, Murphy, Shaw (Luongo 53'), Bannan, Lee (Reach 80'), Harris, Nuhiu (Windass 73'), Wickham.

**Middlesbrough starting eleven:** Stojanovic, Dijksteel,

Fry, Friend, Johnson, Saville, McNair, Spence, Fletcher, Tavernier (Wing 79'), Assombalonga.

# Final Day League Standings

**1 Leeds** (W28, D9, L9, GF77, GA35, PTS 93)
**2 West Brom** (W22, D17, L7, GF77, GA45, PTS 83)
**3** Brentford (W24, D9, L13, GF80, GA38, PTS 81)
**4 Fulham** (W23, D12, L11, GF64, GA48, PTS 81)
**5** Cardiff City (W19, D16, L11, GF68, GA58, PTS 73)
**6** Swansea (W18, D16, L12, GF62, GA53, PTS 70)
**7** Nottm Forest (W18, D16, L12, GF58, GA50, PTS 70)
**8** Millwall (W17, D17, L12, GF57, GA51, PTS 68)
**9** Preston NE (W18, D12, L16, GF59, GA54, PTS 66)
**10** *Derby (W17, D13, L16, GF62, GA64, PTS 64)
**11** Blackburn (W17, D12, L17, GF66, GA63, PTS 63)
**12** Bristol C (W17, D12, L17, GF60, GA65, PTS 63)
**13** QPR (W16, D10, L20, GF67, GA76, PTS 58)
**14** Reading (W15, D11, L20, GF59, GA58, PTS 56)
**15** Stoke (W16, D8, L22, GF62, GA68, PTS 56)
**16** *Sheffield W (W15, D11, L20, GF58, GA66, PTS 56)
**17** Boro (W13, D14, L19, GF48, GA61, PTS 53)
**18** Huddersfield (W13, D12, L21, GF52, GA70, PTS 51)
**19** Luton (W14, D9, L23, GF54, GA82, PTS 51)
**20** Birmingham (W12, D14, L20, GF54, GA75, PTS 50)
**21** Barnsley (W12, D13, L21, GF49, GA69, PTS 49)
**22** Charlton (W12, D12, L22, GF50, GA65, PTS 48)
**23** **Wigan (W15, D14, L17, GF57, GA56, PTS 47)
**24** Hull City (W12, D9, L25, GF57, GA87, PTS 45)

**Play-off final:** Brentford 1-2 **Fulham** (AET)

\* Awaiting verdict of the independent disciplinary commission

\*\* Deducted 12 points for entering into administration (Appeal pending)

League table correct post final day fixtures on the 22$^{nd}$ July 2020

# Sheffield Wednesday's 2019/20 Playing Squad And Contributions

**25** Cameron Dawson (Apps 28, Clean Sheets 10)
**1** Keiren Westwood (Apps 14, Clean Sheets 4)
**28** Joe Wildsmith (Apps 10, Clean Sheets 2)

**27** Dominic Iorfa (Apps 45, Goals 2, Assists 2)
**13** Julian Börner (Apps 40, Goals 1)
**2** Liam Palmer (Apps 34, Assists 1)
**3** Morgan Fox (Apps 32, Goals 3, Assists 1)
**15** Tom Lees (Apps 30, Goals 2, Assists 1)
**22** Moses Odubajo (Apps 24)
**44** Osaze Urhoghide (Apps 4)
**12** Jordan Thorniley (Apps 2)
**26** David Bates (Apps 1)

**7** Kadeem Harris (Apps 47, Goals 3, Assists 5)
**10** Barry Bannan (Apps 46, Goals 2, Assists 8)
**20** Adam Reach (Apps 40, Goals 2, Assists 7)
**5** Kieran Lee (Apps 30, Assists 5)
**21** Massimo Luongo (Apps 30, Goals 3)
**23** Sam Hutchinson (Apps 24, Goals 1, Assists 2)
**8** Joey Pelupessy (Apps 22)
**29** Alex Hunt (Apps 9)
**46** Liam Shaw (Apps 2)

**14** Jacob Murphy (Apps 44, Goals 9, Assists 6)
**17** Atdhe Nuhiu (Apps 41, Goals 7, Assists 4)
**9** Steven Fletcher (Apps 30, Goals 13, Assists 2)
**45** Fernando Forestieri (Apps 19, Goals 2, Assists 2)

**6** Jordan Rhodes (Apps 19, Goals 3)
**11** Sam Winnall (Apps 17, Goals 2, Assists 1)
**38** Alessio Da Cruz (Apps 15, Assists 2)
**19** Connor Wickham (Apps 13, Goals 2)
**47** Josh Windass (Apps 9, Goals 3)
**18** Lucas Joao (Apps 1, Goals 1)

**Top goalscorer:** Steven Fletcher (13)

**Top provider:** Barry Bannan (8)

**Player of the season:** Dominic Iorfa

# POST SEASON

*You Couldn't Write It*

Despite their sixteenth place finish and with all fixtures finalised, Sheffield Wednesday's campaign would still be defined on the verdict of the independent disciplinary commission. The legal battle which started in November was almost in it's ninth month and Wednesday were still unsure if they would be found guilty or cleared of all charges.

The biggest worry was that Sheffield Wednesday would be threatened with relegation if they were to receive a points deduction of at least eight points or more. However, the Owls were not the only side whose fate this term was pending due to outstanding disciplinary cases.

Wigan Athletic completed their season ten points above the drop zone in thirteenth but were handed a twelve point deduction on the final day of the season. This penalty was enforced immediately because they had entered into administration just a few weeks earlier and they now sat almost rock bottom in twenty-third. The Lactics appealed this decision and the result was unresolved, as yet.

Derby County on the other hand had finished fifteen points above the trap door in tenth but were charged by the English Football League succeeding an examination on the sale of their Pride Park stadium. Likewise to the Owls, the Rams strenuously denied any misbehaviour.

With the month of July almost at an end and with both Sheffield Wednesday and the English Football League seemingly confident of a victory, it was expected that the losing party would then appeal against the verdict. Therefore, rumours began to circulate that disciplinary action, if any, could roll on into next term.

It was ever so complicated, these ongoing chain of events felt like it has lasted an age and everyone soon came to realise that it would drag on for just that while longer. It was a case of hoping for the best but expecting the worst. This was the first season in Wednesday's history where their biggest win needed to come off of the field.

Whatever the outcome of the Owls' short-term future, the fans will always continue to love and support Sheffield Wednesday, even if it is just out of curiosity.

Supporting Wednesday this term was another roller-coaster ride and although optimism has been a fundamental trait amongst the Owls faithful for many years, this characteristic is often met with lots of promise but there is always potential for plenty of suffering as the season unfolds. The 2019/20 campaign was no different.

The coronavirus without doubt took centre stage and for the most part was out of everybody's control. There has never been a season like this before and it will forever be remembered due to its intricate nature.

At the start of the season it would've been unimaginable as to how many lives would be lost across the globe due to the pandemic. Nobody could've predicted what was going to happen.

The year 2020 will be recollected for a lifetime and the likelihood is it'll be for all the wrong reasons, but at least that gives us the opportunity to take a moment and reflect. Life is precious.

It is at this point also that we should remind ourselves that football is irrelevant at times and it should never be as important as the health of yourself and that of your loved ones. Still, many Wednesdayites will continue to bleed blue and white.

When expectations are met or exceeded there is an immense feeling of satisfaction and pride, but that is not always the case. The 2019/20 campaign was full of mixed emotions both on and off the field.

In the season where Steve Bruce resigned, Lee Bullen was then put in the caretaker role, Garry Monk was appointed, Fernando Forestieri was handed a six game ban, the Owls were hit with potential misconduct charges, a new decade was entered; and all of this happened prior to the pandemic. It has evidently been one of the strangest of seasons that at one stage looked like it would never be finalised, and all of the above was just the tip of the iceberg.

It is safe to say that the promise of a new decade did not start off with a bang, especially when you consider that the Owls were third in the table at Christmas. Additionally, Sheffield Wednesday had only conjured up one win at Hillsborough since the turn of the year, scoring just five goals in the process and only one of those goals came in the opening forty-five minutes. Also, having beaten QPR in an FA Cup tie in January, and then at a later date in the league, the Owls had won two encounters at the Kiyan Prince Foundation Stadium which was one more than they had won at Hillsborough so far in the entire calender year.

In more ways than one, the Owls' performances on the road this term were much more satisfying. The wins at Middlesbrough, Nottingham Forest, Leeds United and Brighton also all spring to mind.

Other crazy statistics this campaign include the fact that Jordan Rhodes scored all of his goals this season in the space of thirty-seven minutes with a hat-trick at Nottingham Forest. Astonishingly also, Sheffield Wednesday were the lowest home goalscorers in the league with nineteen but were the highest goalscoring team on the road with thirty-nine in total. Honestly, you couldn't write it.

When it was declared that the 2020/21 term was set to commence on the weekend of 12th September, there was only a seven-week turnaround between then and the start of next season. Because of this, it was difficult to see how the Owls could prepare or plan in advance when Wednesday's legal conflict with the English Football League was still inconclusive. Still, some objectives should remain the same. The Chairman, management staff and players all have their work cut ahead of next season and the main focus has to be on the bigger picture of Sheffield Wednesday as a football club.

Signing or promoting youth in hope to find a player with that indefinable magic and developing an inspiring culture are just a couple of indispensable recommendations. All the same, both of these are influenced by so many variables and it would be unrealistic to think that any of this will happen overnight. The hard work never stops.

With all of that in mind and when the transfer window opened on the 27th July for the minimum ten-week period, it was just one day later when Garry Monk captured his first summer signing. Fisayo Dele-Bashiru joined the Owls from Manchester City for an undisclosed fee. The nineteen-year-old had penned a three-year deal at Hillsborough and he certainly fit the mould of the young ambitious player that Monk was searching for.

It was almost guaranteed that Bashiru wouldn't be the last arrival in the next few months, especially when you consider how threadbare Wednesday's squad was compared to this time last year. Ahead of next season and with the possibility of a shake-up in the back-room staff too, there would be no room for failure on the recruitment front.

## The Verdict

On Friday the 31$^{st}$ July at 7pm, eight-months and seventeen-days after the initial charge, Sheffield Wednesday received their first ever points deduction. The independent disciplinary commission had found the Owls guilty of breaching profitability and spending rules, this was because they should not have included the profits from the sale of Hillsborough stadium dated within the financial documents for the closing period of July 2018.

This sanction stated that a twelve point penalty would be imposed at the start of the 2020/21 campaign. However, the independent disciplinary commission did conclude that Sheffield Wednesday were innocent of any aggravated breach. This could've seen the Owls hit with a further deduction of up-to nine points. Anyhow, the club were cleared of any wrongdoing on this part.

The Owls addressed the judgement made by the commission but still desired further clarity on their decision. Once the club had visual of the written verdict they would have fourteen-days to appeal if they decided to do so.

Just when you thought Garry Monk had a tough job on his hands, it was now going to be harder than ever before. The Wednesday boss had previously managed under imposed deductions at Birmingham City in the 2018/19 campaign and the Blues respectfully finished seventeenth that season. Monk had done it before and he would have to do it all again.

As this news sent shock-waves throughout the fanbase, one saving grace was the fact that this punishment was not inflicted this term which would've consequently seen the Owls fall to the bottom of the table and relegated to League One. Still, many people were angered by this decision.

If Wednesday had been handed a twelve point deduction this season, Charlton Athletic, who occupied twenty-second in the standings would've climbed one place and moved out of the relegation zone. The Addicks were quick to threaten legal action as they awaited answers from the English Football League before making a move.

For what it's worth, it was impossible for the independent disciplinary commission to do a U-turn on their ruling. Wednesday would not get a points deduction this term because the English Football League season had officially ended on the completion of each final day fixture.

The can of worms was wide open and even though the footballing season was over, there was still a possibility of a change in the league standings. Both Wigan's appeal and Derby's legal proceedings were still undetermined. Even so, similar to the Owls it was almost certain that any sanctions imposed on Derby would be carried over to next season.

Whatever the outcome of these cases, this was the first season that Sheffield Wednesday were not promoted or relegated at the turn of a new decade since the 1959/60 campaign. Wednesday had avoided the drop by the skin of their teeth.

It was then in the following week on the 4th August when Wigan Athletic's relegation to League One was confirmed. Their appeal over a twelve point deduction was dismissed and the league table would remain as it was post fixtures on the 22nd July. Barnsley, who would've been relegated if Wigan's appeal was successful were now certain of their Championship survival, and this also meant that Sheffield Wednesday did finish in sixteenth position after all.

In the same week when all of the Owls first-team players returned for pre-season training, Friday the 14th August, a huge decision was still to be made. Would Wednesday appeal against the twelve point penalty made by the independent disciplinary commission?

If they decided to do so it would take a further two-weeks minimum before a judgement was made. Otherwise, the Owls may decide to just grin and bare it, but that was unlikely.

After the extraordinary and unprecedented season that Wednesday had just completed, it was almost indisputable that there would be more twists and turns still to come. You would've thought that a conclusion was near with the new league term just four-weeks away, wouldn't you?

As it stands, Sheffield Wednesday would live to fight another day in the Championship but this time they would have a huge deficit to overhaul. Survival would be the number one priority. It was going to be one hell of a challenge, but that's not to say it's impossible.

Here's to a successful and momentous 2020/21 season...

# ABOUT THE AUTHOR

## Louis Paul Shackshaft

Louis was born in South Yorkshire and fell in love with Sheffield Wednesday at a young age thanks to John Sheridan's League Cup winning goal against Manchester United in 1991.

In later life, having always had a passion for football and writing, he completed his BA Honours Degree in Sports Studies and Sports Journalism Diploma. Consequently, Louis' football writing journey began when he started reporting on the Owls for Shoot football in 2015.

Since then, as a freelance football writer, other work and contributions have included many regional and national publications; he was also a finalist at the Football Content Awards in the category 'Best New Football Blog'. In addition, Louis hosts the Championship Round-Table Podcast, a weekly discussion on English footballs second tier.

Web: louisshackshaft.com Twitter: @LouisShackshaft

# BIBLIOGRAPHY

**Websites**

www.swfc.co.uk (Sheffield Wednesday Football Club)

www.efl.com (English Football League)

www.11v11.com (Football History and Statistics)

www.transfermarkt.co.uk (Statistics)

www.whoscored.com (Statistics)

Printed in Great Britain
by Amazon

23127350R00088